Mom'n'Pop's Apple Pie

1950s Cookbook

Mom 'n' Pop's Apple Pie

1950s Cookbook

Over 300 Great Recipes from the Golden Age of American Home Cooking

Compiled and Edited by Barbara Stuart Peterson

SMITHMARK

Table of Contents

Copyright © 1997
American Graphic Systems, Inc.

All rights reserved. No part of this publication
may be reproduced, stored in a retrieval system
or transmitted in any form by any means, elec-
tronic, mechanical, photocopying or otherwise,
without first obtaining written permission of the
copyright owner.

This edition published in 1997
by SMITHMARK Publishers, Inc.
a division of U.S. Media Holdings, Inc.
16 East 32nd Street
New York, NY 10016

SMITHMARK books are available for bulk pur-
chase for sales promotion and premium use. For
details write or telephone the Manager of Special
Sales, SMITHMARK Publishers Inc., a division of
U.S. Media Holdings, Inc., 16 East 32nd Street,
New York, NY 10016. (212) 532-6600.

Produced by American Graphic Systems, Inc.
P.O. Box 460313
San Francisco, CA 94146

Designed by Bill Yenne, with design assistance
from Azia Yenne. Proofreading by Amy Bokser,
Joan Hayes and Andy Roe.

ISBN 0-765-194996

Printed in Hong Kong

10 9 8 7 6 5 4 3 2 1

Picture credits:
All pictures are from the American Graphic Systems
collection, with the following exceptions:

Alvarado Historic Collection: pages 1, 2, 10, 11, 14,
    27, 34, 36, 40, 44, 48, 52, 59, 66, 72,
    74, 76, 79, 84, 88, 89, 93, 97, 101,
    104, 109, 112
American Egg Board: page 96
American Lamb Council: pages 29, 80, 81, 85
The J.R. Fratelli Cinema Collection: pages 82, 83
Florida Tomatoes: pages 20, 25, 37, 49, 53
National Broiler Council: pages 45, 56, 57, 61, 64,
    65, 68, 69
National Cattleman's Beef Association: pages 15, 41
National Live Stock and Meat Board: pages 24, 28,
    32, 33, 73, 76- 77
The Sierra Solana Library: pages 6, 7, 12
Stock Editions: pages 17, 92, 105, 108
Wheat Foods Council: pages 21, 60, 100

Introduction
by
Barbara Stuart Peterson

This book is a celebration of a time when life was simpler, and perhaps better. It was a time when our families still gathered around the dinner table every day for wholesome home-cooked meals.

This book is a celebration of the foods, and of the lifestyle that we enjoyed in the 1950s. These are the foods that I remember from my childhood and which I have prepared for my own family in the decades since. These recipes, collected over many years, evoke the 1950s, and they are the types of foods that were served on my mom's dinner table, or on the backyard picnic table next to my pop's grill.

The 1950s were a time of unprecedented prosperity for Americans, and this made it possible for a unique lifestyle to develop. Women, who had entered the work force in unprecedented numbers during World War II, could now become full-time homemakers, and more women than ever before in history became homemakers in new homes.

The decade after World War II saw the construction of more new single family houses than ever before.

Developers created vast suburbs on previously open land around major cities, and found a ready market in the young families whose children came to be known as the "baby boomers."

The era of prosperity also made these homes a new and exciting place. The homemakers of the 1950s could still remember wood-burning kitchen stoves and refrigerators that were literally "ice boxes," in which keeping the milk cold was dependent on slabs of ice purchased from the ice man. By 1950, however, the average American kitchen had changed dramatically from what it had been in the prewar years. Gas and electric ranges had entirely replaced wood stoves. Electric refrigerators, which were relatively rare before World War II, quickly evolved. For example, the racks on the inside of the door went from being a major innovation to standard equipment, and the automatic ice maker became available.

Prosperity made it possible for people with prewar kitchens to upgrade, and of course, all the new tract housing that was being put up came equipped with thoroughly "modern" kitchens. The cost of electricity, driven down by the great hydroelectric developments of the 1930s and the prediction of unlimited energy from the new nuclear plants, led to the promise of the "all-electric kitchen." This was a dream that the mothers of the 1950s housewives would never have imagined in their younger years.

In these new kitchens, the homemakers of the 1950s fashioned meals that were a blend of what they had learned from their moms from women's magazines and from swapping recipes with friends across the backyard fence. At our house, grandma's old favorites were still a staple in our diet, but mom was willing to try something new from the spice drawer once in a while.

I remember when mom started to use garlic, and the first time she used tarragon on

In the 1950s, kitchens were a happy, cheerful, family environment.

During the 1950s, we also gathered in the backyard for barbeques, and to chat with the neighbors.

chicken dinner. Pop said it smelled like Thanksgiving, and we all loved it.

In the 1950s, the lifestyle of many suburban families included the backyard grill, and that somehow became pop's domain. On those sunny summer days, he would don his chef's hat and throw some burgers on the coals. When she saw pop at the backyard grill, grandma always reminded us with a wink that grandpa had never lifted a finger to cook anything.

The 1950s were really the golden age of American home cooking. The new kitchens allowed the young moms to cook the recipes they had learned from their moms and grandmothers with ease, and the unprecedented array of labor-saving kitchen appliances gave them time to experiment a little bit without straying too far from the basics. The 1950s were an era when packaged foods meant canned peas. The concept of entire packaged meals (we called them "TV dinners") was invented in the 1950s, but few people resorted to these more than once a week until the 1960s.

In the 1950s, we saw the meals that mom put on the table as being truly American. In the 1960s, when "foreign" food, such as pizza, started to be common, I remember pop saying that the only two foreign foods he had ever tasted were Swiss cheese and French fries. It is certainly true that our diets were much more limited then. Almost no one had ever tasted a taco, and

pizza was something that you could find only in the Italian neighborhoods of larger cities. Terminology was also different. The word "pasta" had not yet entered our vocabulary. Noodles were noodles, and macaroni came with elbows or it came shaped like letters in our "alphabet" soup.

However limited they may have been, the basic foods were better back then. A home-made hot dish is <u>always</u> better than anything that you find pre-packaged in the frozen food section. Just because we don't have as much time as mom did to prepare our meals, doesn't mean that we can't enjoy a good home-cooked meal once in a while, and that's what this book is all about.

In this book, we return to those wonderful days of bean salad, baked beans and green bean casseroles. We have selected recipes that recapture a spirit of simplicity and of wholesomeness. These recipes were chosen with an eye to the recipes that mom inherited from grandma, ones she developed herself and ones which capture the spirit of those times. In most cases, these are oven or stove top meals, although in some cases we have also included microwave instructions where they seem appropriate.

Whether you grew up in the 1950s or the 1980s, I hope that you'll enjoy this book and find recipes that help evoke a time and a table where the food was cooked fresh and cleaning up our plates was a joy.

Mom'n'Pop's
Appetizers and Salads

Mom's Meat 'n' Cheese Ball

Serves 4

Ingredients:

2	packages	(8 ounces) cream cheese
1	package	(10 ounces) sharp cheddar cheese
1	teaspoon	Worcestershire sauce
2	packages	(3 ounces), chopped shredded, dried beef
½	cup	chopped pimento olives

Directions:

Combine all of the above and mix well. Shape into a ring or ball. Serve with crackers or party breads. This can be made into two balls rolled in pecans and used at a later date.

Mom's Favorite Cheese Log

Serves 10

Ingredients:

½	pound	sharp cheddar cheese
2	teaspoons	Worcestershire sauce
½	pound	pimento cheese
¼	teaspoon	red pepper
½	pound	cream cheese
2	tablespoons	mayonnaise
2		garlic cloves
¼	teaspoon	salt

Directions:

Grate cheese. Add all ingredients. Chill a little and divide into thirds. Roll in paprika.
Note: Your log may be frozen.

Easy Cream Cheese Ball

Serves 5

Ingredients:

8	ounces	cream cheese, softened
1	tablespoon	milk
1	package	corned/chipped beef cut in strips with scissors
		chopped ripe/green olives
½	cup	ground nuts

salt and pepper to taste

Directions:

Add the milk to the softened cream cheese first. Blend all ingredients together. Roll in ground nuts for ball. Cool and spread on crackers.

Everybody Likes Oven Fries

Serves 4

Ingredients:

6		medium potatoes
2	tablespoons	oil
1	ounce	Italian dressing mix
1	tablespoon	chopped fresh parsley

Directions:

Preheat your oven to 350F. Peel potatoes and slice for french fries. Lay out on paper towel, pat dry. Potatoes should be as dry as possible. Put potatoes in a large bowl and drizzle with oil, tossing to coat evenly. Lay in a single layer on a large baking sheet. Sprinkle dry dressing mix and parsley over all. Bake 25 minutes, then flip over only once. Return to oven and increase temperature to 450F. Cook 3 to 5 minutes longer until potatoes are tender and start to brown.

Deviled Eggs

Courtesy of The American Egg Board
Serves 6

Ingredients:

6		hard-cooked eggs*
2	tablespoons	bottled low calorie or light Italian-style salad dressing
½	teaspoon	prepared mustard
1	jar (2 oz.)	chopped pimento, drained
1	tablespoon	chopped fresh mushrooms
1	tablespoon	chopped green pepper

Directions:

Cut eggs in half lengthwise. Remove yolks and set whites aside. Mash yolks with fork. Blend in dressing and mustard. Stir in remaining ingredients. Refill whites using about 1 tablespoon yolk mixture for each egg half. Chill to blend flavors, if desired.

*To hard-cook: Put eggs in single layer in saucepan. Add enough tap water to come at least one inch above eggs. Cover and quickly bring just to boiling. Turn off heat. If necessary, remove pan from burner to prevent further boiling. Let eggs stand covered in the hot water 15 to 17 minutes for large eggs. (Adjust time up or down by about three minutes for each size larger or smaller.) Immediately run cold water over eggs or put them in ice water until completely cooled. To remove shell, crack it by tapping gently all over. Roll egg between hands to loosen shell, then peel, starting at large end. Hold egg under running cold water or dip in bowl of water to help ease off shell.

Deviled Eggs 'n' Chicken

Serves 6

Ingredients:

6		hard cooked eggs
½	cup	finely chopped, cooked chicken
3	tablespoons	mayonnaise
1	tablespoon	grated onion
1	teaspoon	Dijon mustard
½	teaspoon	dry mustard
¾	teaspoon	hot pepper sauce, to taste
1	tablespoon	minced parsley paprika, for garnish

Directions:

1. Hard cook eggs and remove shells. Cut eggs lengthwise in half. Remove yolks and place them in a small bowl.

2. Mash yolks with a fork. Add chicken, mayonnaise, onion, Dijon mustard, dry mustard, hot sauce and parsley. Blend well. Stuff egg whites with yolk mixture. Sprinkle tops with paprika to garnish. Cover and refrigerate until serving time.

Noodles with Deviled Eggs

Serves 4

Ingredients:

1		batch of deviled eggs
2	tablespoons	chopped onion
1	tablespoon	margarine or butter
2½	cups	noodles, cooked
1	cup	(8 ounces) dairy sour cream
½	cup	grated parmesan cheese
½	cup	milk
½	cup	sliced ripe olives
2	teaspoons	poppy seeds
½	teaspoon	salt

Directions:

Prepare deviled eggs according to recipe. Cover and microwave onion and margarine in 1½-quart casserole on high (100 percent) until onion is tender, 1½ to 2 minutes. Stir in remaining ingredients, except eggs. Cover and microwave until hot, 5 to 6 minutes. Arrange eggs on noodles. Cover and microwave until eggs are hot, 1 to 2 minutes.

Old-Fashioned Orange Gelatin Salad

Serves 20

Ingredients:

1	package	orange flavored gelatin, large
1	package	small curd cottage cheese, large
1	package	Whipped topping

Directions:

In a serving dish or casserole, mix a large box of dry flavored gelatin mix with a large container of small curd cottage cheese. Mix thoroughly until flavored gelatin is dissolved. Fold in large container of whipped topping. Blend thoroughly. Chill thoroughly. Garnish with mint leaves or mandarin orange slices. This recipe is also great with peach flavored gelatin. A combination of peach and orange is also another alternative (a small box of each). If you make the peach salad, you can add crushed pineapple (drained) for a fruity salad.

Grandma's Cobb Salad

Serves 4

Ingredients:

6	cups	finely shredded lettuce
2	cups	cut-up cooked chicken
3		hard-cooked eggs, chopped
2	medium	tomatoes, chopped (1½ cups)
1		ripe avocado, chopped
¼	cup	crumbled blue cheese (1 ounce)
4	slices	bacon, crisp and crumbled

Lemon vinaigrette:

½	cup	vegetable oil
¼	cup	lemon juice
1	tablespoon	red wine vinegar
2	teaspoons	sugar
½	teaspoon	salt
½	teaspoon	dry mustard
½	teaspoon	Worcestershire sauce
¼	teaspoon	garlic powder
¼	teaspoon	pepper

Directions:

Prepare lemon vinaigrette: Shake all ingredients in tightly covered container. Divide lettuce among 4 salad plates or bowls. Arrange remaining ingredients in rows on lettuce. Serve with lemon vinaigrette. Refrigerate at least one hour.

Home-Made Cole Slaw

Serves 10

Ingredients:

5	tablespoons	mayonnaise (heaping)
1	teaspoon	hot sauce
2	tablespoons	yellow mustard (heaping)
2	tablespoons	ketchup
2	tablespoons	olive oil
1	tablespoon	wine vinegar
1	teaspoon	garlic salt
1	tablespoon	Worcestershire sauce
3	teaspoons	salt (to taste)
4		bell peppers, sliced
2		onions, medium, shredded
1		large cabbage, shredded

juice of medium size lemon

Directions:

Put mayonnaise and mustard in a bowl large enough to hold complete mixture, but shaped so that the mixture can be beaten with a fork. Beat mayonnaise and mustard until combined. Add olive oil slowly, beating all the time. Beat until mixture has returned to the thickness of mayonnaise. Add hot sauce, continuing to beat. Add ketchup and keep beating. Add salt and garlic salt, beating all the time. Add wine vinegar. (This will thin the sauce down). Beat this thoroughly, adding the lemon juice as you do so. Taste for salt and pepper. Place

When the kids were staying over at friends' houses, mom 'n' pop had to eat alone.

shredded cabbage, peppers, and onions in a large salad bowl. Pour sauce over them and toss well. This should be done about an hour before serving. Tastes even better the next day.

Easy Macaroni Salad

Serves 6

Ingredients:

2½	quarts	boiling water
2	cups	macaroni or tiny shells
1	teaspoon	oil
2	teaspoons	salt
¾	cup	mayonnaise
2	teaspoons	pimento, chopped
2	teaspoons	green onion
2	teaspoons	sweet pickle, chopped
1	teaspoon	sugar
1	teaspoon	mustard, prepared
½	teaspoon	seasoned salt
¼	teaspoon	pepper
¼	teaspoon	paprika

Television made family dinner hour so much more fun.

Directions:

In large uncovered dutch oven cook macaroni in boiling water, cooking oil, and salt until tender but firm, about 5 to 7 minutes. Drain. Rinse with cold water. Drain well again. Return macaroni to pot. Combine the rest of the ingredients in a small bowl. Mix well. Add to macaroni. Toss together well. Place in a serving bowl. Chill for one hour or more. If you want it more moist, add a bit of milk.

Our Three-Bean Salad

Serves 6

Ingredients:

1	16 ounce can	green beans, drained
1	16 ounce can	wax beans, drained
1	16 ounce can	kidney beans, drained
4		green onions (with tops), chopped (about ¼ cup)
¼	cup	chopped fresh parsley
1	cup	Italian dressing
1	tablespoon	sugar
2	cloves	garlic, crushed

Directions:

Mix beans, onions and parsley. Separately mix Italian dressing, sugar and garlic. Pour over bean mixture and toss. Cover and refrigerate at least 3 hours, stirring occasionally.

Mom's Cooked Bean Salad

Serves 4

Ingredients:

1	cup	cooked pinto beans
1	cup	cooked navy beans
1	cup	cooked red kidney beans
1		celery stalk, diced
1		green bell pepper, diced
2		garlic cloves, diced
½	cup	oil
2	tablespoons	apple cider vinegar
1	tablespoon	light molasses
3	tablespoons	nutritional yeast
½	teaspoon	salt
½	teaspoon	garlic powder
¼	teaspoon	paprika
¼	teaspoon	oregano
¼	teaspoon	basil
¼	teaspoon	ground red pepper

Directions:

Combine beans and diced vegetables in a large bowl. Place remaining ingredients in blender and blend on high for 1 minute. Add to bean vegetable mixture. Season to taste. Blend more seasoned liquid if desired. Chill for 2 hours.

Just Green Bean Salad

Serves 6

Ingredients:

3	pounds	fresh green beans
3	medium	onions, thinly sliced
1		egg
¼	cup	olive oil
¼	cup	lemon juice
2	cloves	garlic, minced
¼	teaspoon	dry mustard
		black pepper to taste

Directions:

Put a large pot of water on to boil. In the meantime, wash the green beans, and when the water comes to a boil, let the green beans cook for about 5 minutes, until soft. Drain the water and cool the beans. In a blender, add the egg, olive oil, lemon juice, garlic, and mustard. Blend well. In a salad bowl, place cooked green beans with onions. Pour the dressing over it, and sprinkle with black pepper.

Mom's Ham 'n' Beet Salad

Serves 6

Ingredients:

3		eggs
2	medium	cooked beets
2	tablespoons	oil
1	tablespoon	vinegar
1 to 2		apples
½	pound	cooked ham, cut in cubes
1	slice	lettuce
1		lemon (garnish)
		seasonings of choice
		cocktail onions and/or olives

Directions:

Hard cook the eggs. Crack the shells. Keep one egg for garnish. Halve the other two eggs. Remove the yolks. Chop the yolks and whites separately. Do not chop too finely. Peel and cut the beets in slices, and then into match sticks. Put into a bowl with the oil, vinegar, and seasonings. Peel the apples and cut into neat pieces. Add to the beets with the diced ham. Mix the egg yolks and whites with the beets. Pile onto a bed of lettuce. Garnish with rings of hard cooked egg, lemon and the onion and/or olives. Serve with fresh bread or rolls. This also makes an excellent hors d'oeuvre for 6-8 people, particularly good if fish is the main course. Store in refrigerator. Vary by omitting apple, and adding cooked rice or diced, cooked potato.

New refrigerators were considered glamorous in the 1950s.

Pop's Potato Salad

Serves 24

Ingredients:

10	pounds	potatoes
8		eggs, hard-boiled
2	cups	dill relish
1	cup	sweet relish
2	cups	salad olives, chopped
2	cups	onions, finely chopped
1	cup	celery, finely chopped
1	cup	fresh parsley, finely chopped
1½	pints	mayonnaise
½	cup	yellow mustard
		salt, to taste
1		hot sauce

Directions:

Boil potatoes in their jackets. Let cool, then peel and chop into large chunks. Mix mayonnaise, yellow mustard, hot sauce, and salt together. Add potatoes, along with the rest of the ingredients, and mix well. You can make this the day before and refrigerate it overnight. Add more dressing if it is too dry.

Old-Time Cabbage Salad

Serves 4

Ingredients:

5		bacon slices
1	teaspoon	sugar
2	tablespoons	vinegar
¼	cup	wine, red or white
½		red cabbage head, shredded
2	tablespoons	vegetable oil
½	teaspoon	salt
¼	teaspoon	pepper
1	tablespoon	caraway seeds

Directions:

Fry bacon in a medium sized frying pan until crisp. Remove and reserve bacon drippings. Add sugar, vinegar, and wine to bacon fat. Stir and cook until sugar is dissolved. Pour this hot mixture over the cabbage. Toss with vegetable oil, salt, pepper, and caraway seeds. Sprinkle crumbled bacon over mixture. Serve at room temperature.

Grandma's Five-Bean Salad

Serves 10

Ingredients:

1	cup	sugar
½	teaspoon	salt
1	cup	vinegar
16	ounces	green beans, canned, drained
16	ounces	yellow beans, canned, drained
16	ounces	lima beans, canned, drained
16	ounces	garbanzo beans, canned, drained
16	ounces	red kidney beans, canned, drained
1		green pepper, slivered
4		celery ribs, sliced
3		onions, medium, sliced thin

Directions:

Combine sugar, salt, and vinegar in a pan. Bring to a boil for 1 minute. Cool. Toss all other ingredients together and pour the vinegar mixture over them. Marinate for 24 hours in refrigerator, stirring occasionally.

Mom's Potato Salad

Serves 6

Ingredients:

6		potatoes, large
½	teaspoon	salt
1		onion, medium, minced
3	tablespoons	vinegar
½	teaspoon	mustard, prepared
1	teaspoon	sugar
2	teaspoons	dill seed

Directions:

Potatoes should be peeled and quartered. In medium saucepan cook potatoes in boiling, salted water until tender. Drain, reserving ¾ cup of potato water. Dice potatoes. Add oil and minced onion. Toss gently. In small saucepan bring the ¾ cup potato water to a boil. Pour over potatoes and onion. Keep at room temperature for 2 to 3 hours. Stir in vinegar, mustard, sugar, and dill seed. Potato salad will be creamy. Serve at room temperature.

Mom'n'Pop's
Burgers, Hot Dogs and Sandwiches

Pop's Barbeque Burgers

Serves 6

Ingredients:

1½	pounds	ground beef
½	cup	onion, chopped (1 medium)
1	teaspoon	salt
½	cup	ketchup
½	cup	chili sauce
2	tablespoons	brown sugar
1	tablespoon	lemon juice

Directions:

Mix the meat, onion, and salt together. Shape the mixture into 6 patties, each about ¾ inch thick. Brown the patties in a large skillet over medium high heat, turning once. Cover and cook over low heat about 10 minutes. Drain off the excess fat. Mix ketchup, chili sauce, brown sugar, and lemon juice. Pour sauce over the patties. Cover and simmer for 15 minutes, spooning the sauce onto the patties occasionally. Serve with the sauce spooned over the patties.

The Best Burgers

Courtesy of The National Cattleman's Beef Association

Serves 6

Ingredients:

2	pounds	ground beef (80 percent lean)
1	teaspoon	salt
¼	teaspoon	pepper
6		large hamburger buns, toasted

tomatoes, thinly sliced
onions, thinly sliced
lettuce leaves
pickle slices
American cheese slices, or
            processed cheese spread, warmed
ketchup
mustard

Sometimes pop didn't pay attention to his grilling.

The Best Burgers are always a result of first class beef and paying attention to the grill.

Directions:
Combine ground beef, salt, and pepper, mixing lightly but thoroughly. Divide beef mixture into 6 equal portions; shape into ½ inch thick patties, 4 inches in diameter. Place patties on rack in broiler pan so surface of meat is 3 to 4 inches from heat. Broil 20 minutes or to desired doneness, turning once. Place cooked burgers in buns; garnish with desired choice of toppings.

Grilling directions: Place beef patties on grill over medium coals.* Grill 7 to 9 minutes or to desired doneness, turning once. Serve in buns with desired toppings as directed above.

*To check temperature, cautiously hold hand about 4 inches above coals. Medium coals will force removal of hand in 4 seconds.

Cheeseburgers 'n' Chili

Serves 6

Ingredients:

1½	pounds	ground beef
¼	cup	onion, finely chopped (1 small)
1	teaspoon	chili powder
1	teaspoon	Worcestershire sauce
¾	teaspoon	salt
¼	teaspoon	garlic salt
¼	teaspoon	pepper
¼	teaspoon	red pepper sauce
6		cheddar cheese slices
2	tablespoons	green chilies, canned, chopped
1	dash	cayenne red pepper

Directions:

Mix all the ingredients together except the cheese slices and chilies. Shape the mixture into 12 thin patties, each about 3½ inches in diameter. Place 1 cheese slice and 1 teaspoon of the chilies on each of 6 patties. Top with the remaining 6 patties, sealing the edges firmly. Broil or grill the patties 4 inches from the heat, turning once, until the desired doneness is reached, about 10 to 15 minutes.

Grandma's Home-Made Burger and Hot Dog Relish

Serves 8

Ingredients:

3	pounds	sweet red peppers
3	pounds	sweet green peppers*
3	pounds	onions, peeled
4	cups	cider vinegar
½	cup	sugar
1	teaspoon	mustard seeds
1	teaspoon	dry mustard
1	teaspoon	celery seeds
2	tablespoons	salt

Directions:

Put the vegetables through the medium blade of a food chopper. Cover the vegetables with boiling water, let stand for 15 minutes, and drain well. Add the remaining ingredients, bring to a boil and cook for 10 minutes, stirring occasionally. Place in hot jars and seal.
* Peppers should be seeded.

East Coast Hot Dogs

Serves 4 to 6

Ingredients:

½	cup	water
1		medium onion, sliced or chopped
½	cup	ketchup
4	tablespoons	cider vinegar
1	teaspoon	dry mustard
1	teaspoon	paprika
		freshly ground pepper
6		foot-long hot dogs

Directions:

In saucepan combine water, onion, ketchup, vinegar, dry mustard, paprika, and pepper. Bring to a boil. Reduce heat. Simmer 5 minutes. Arrange hot dogs side by side in shallow 9 x 9 inch pan. Cover with onion mixture and bake in a 350F oven for 30-40 minutes.

Pop's Favorite Corn Dogs

Serves 6

Ingredients:

½	cup	yellow corn meal
½	cup	flour
1	teaspoon	dry mustard
½	teaspoon	salt
1		egg, lightly beaten
6		skewers or sticks
6		frankfurters
1	tablespoon	sugar
1	teaspoon	baking powder
½	cup	milk
1	tablespoon	melted shortening

Directions:

Combine the cornmeal, flour, sugar, mustard, baking powder, and salt, mixing well. Add the milk, egg and shortening, mixing until very smooth. Pour the mixture into a tall glass. Put the frankfurters on sticks. Dip them into the cornmeal batter to coat them evenly. Deep fry in oil heated to 375F until golden brown, about two minutes. Drain on paper towels.

Mom 'n' Pop and the kids always enjoyed a good old All-American hot dog.

Hot Dog 'n' Cheese

Serves 10

Ingredients:

30		cocktail franks
10		cheese slices
2	packages	crescent rolls

Directions:

Take the roll dough and unroll carefully. Cut each triangle in half (you will need part of the second package, but not all), keeping the triangular shape. Then wrap ¼ of a piece of cheese around the frank and, holding it with your fingers, start rolling it in the roll. Start at the large end of the triangle and roll towards the tip. Bake in a hot oven until brown. This should take only about 10 minutes at 400F. Watch carefully. Take out when browned and serve them immediately.

Pop's Quick Grilled Cheese

Serves 4

Ingredients:

12	slices	processed American cheese
8	slices	white or whole wheat bread
		margarine or butter, softened

Directions:

Place half of the cheese on 4 slices of bread. Top with remaining bread. Spread top slices of bread with margarine or butter. Place sandwiches, margarine or butter sides down, in skillet. Spread tops of bread with margarine or butter. Cook uncovered over medium heat about 5 minutes, or until golden brown. Turn over and continue heating 2 to 3 minutes or until golden brown and cheese is melted.

Home-Made Chicken Salad

Serves 6

Ingredients:

3	cups	cooked chicken, cubed
1	pound	steamed asparagus
½		pineapple, cubed and steamed or
1	can(20 ounce)	pineapple chunks, drained
2		tomatoes, sliced
1		onion diced
1		green pepper, sliced
1	can (7 ounce)	green olives, sliced
1	tablespoon	parsley, chopped
1	tablespoon	basil
1	head	iceberg lettuce, torn

Directions:

Combine all ingredients and toss with dressing of your choice. Put on sandwich bread or roll.

Mom'n'Pop's
Biscuits, Muffins and Breads

Grandma's Country Biscuits

Serves 6

Ingredients:

2	cups	flour
2½	teaspoons	double-acting baking powder
2	teaspoons	sugar
1	teaspoon	salt
7	tablespoons	butter
¾	cup	milk

Directions:

Preheat the oven to 375F. Combine all the dry ingredients in a large bowl. Cut the butter into small bits and stir them into the dry ingredients, using your finger tips or a pastry cutter to make sure it's well combined. Next, slowly add the milk to the mixture while stirring continually. Once the milk has been added, knead the dough for one minute until smooth. Roll the dough out to a ¼ inch thickness. Cut into squares and place on a dry cookie sheet. Place the cookie sheet on the middle rack of the oven. Bake for 12 minutes.

Good Old-Fashioned Buttermilk Biscuits

Serves 18

Ingredients:

3	cups	flour, all-purpose, sifted
1	teaspoon	salt
½	teaspoon	baking soda
3	teaspoons	baking powder
¾	cups	shortening
1	cup	buttermilk
4	tablespoons	butter (optional)

Directions:
1. Preheat your oven to 450F
2. Sift flour, salt, baking soda, and baking powder into mixing bowl. Cut in shortening, using 2 knives or a pastry cutter. Your hands should be dusted with flour. Add sufficient buttermilk to make a soft dough. Knead lightly and turn out onto a lightly floured board. Roll out to ½ an inch thickness and cut with biscuit cutter into rounds. Place rounds not touching, for crisper biscuits or close together, for softer biscuits, on ungreased baking sheet. Brush with melted butter if desired. Bake in preheated oven 12-15 minutes, or until firm and lightly browned.

Easy Baking Powder Biscuits

Serves 6

Ingredients:

3	cups	ready-mixed flour
7	tablespoons	shortening
1	cup	milk

Directions:

Sift flour, measure, and sift again. Cut in shortening with 2 spatulas. Add milk. Turn onto lightly floured board. Knead lightly and pat into sheet ½ inch thick. Cut with floured cutter. Bake in hot oven (450F) 12 minutes.

Mom's Buttermilk Biscuits

Serves 6

Ingredients:

2	cups	unbleached all-purpose flour
2¼	teaspoons	baking powder
1	teaspoon	salt
¼	teaspoon	baking soda
6	tablespoons	butter
¾	cup	buttermilk

Directions:

Mix flour and other ingredients, adding the butter and the buttermilk last. Mix quickly, and put on a floured board. Knead lightly a few seconds. Roll out to a ½ inch thickness, cut biscuits, and put on a buttered baking sheet. Bake at 450F for 12-15 minutes.

Home-Style Apple Bread

Serves 6

Ingredients:

½	cup	butter or margarine
½	cup	sugar
2		eggs, beaten
1	tablespoon	lemon juice
2	cups	flour
1	teaspoon	baking powder
½	teaspoon	salt
2	cups	chopped, peeled apples
1	cup	chopped black walnuts or pecans

Directions:

Preheat your oven to 350F. Cream butter, sugar, eggs, and lemon juice. Stir in flour, baking powder, and salt. Fold in apples and nuts. Bake in a greased and floured 9 x 5 x 3 inch loaf pan for 45-55 minutes.

Apple-Cheese Corn Muffins

Serves 12

Ingredients:

1 ½	cups	flour
1 ½	ounces	uncooked yellow corn meal
1	tablespoon	baking powder
¾	pound	apples, cored, pared, finely chopped before cutting
½	cup	corn
2 ¼	ounces	shredded cheddar cheese
¼	cup	sugar
1	dash	cinnamon
1	dash	nutmeg
¼	cup	corn oil
3		eggs, lightly beaten

Directions:

1. Preheat your oven to 400F. Line 12 muffin pan cups with paper baking cups.
2. In large bowl combine flour, cornmeal, and baking powder. Add apples, corn, cheese, sugar, cinnamon and nutmeg, stirring to combine. In small bowl, beat eggs and oil. Stir into flour mixture. (Do not overbeat. The mixture will be stiff.)

3. Fill baking cups and bake in center of oven for 15 minutes. Makes 12 muffins.

Mom's Apple Muffins

Serves 4

Ingredients:

½	cup	shortening
½	cup	sugar, granulated
2		eggs, large
1 ½	cups	unbleached flour
1	teaspoon	baking soda
1	teaspoon	baking powder
½	teaspoon	salt
¾	cup	oats, quick cooking
1	cup	apples, finely chopped
½	cup	cheddar, sharp, coarsely grated
½	cup	pecans, chopped
¾	cup	milk
		apple slices*
		butter, melted
		cinnamon-sugar mixture

Directions:

Preheat the oven to 400F. Cream the shortening and sugar together and add the eggs one at a time, beating well after each addition. Combine the flour, baking powder, baking soda, and salt in a mixing bowl. Mix lightly. Gradually stir the flour mixture into the shortening mixture. In this order, add the oats, cheddar and pecans, mixing well after each addition. Gradually add the milk, stirring until all the ingredients are just moistened. Grease the muffin pans and fill each cup half full of batter. Dip the apple slices in the melted butter and then into the cinnamon-sugar. Press 1 apple slice into the top of each muffin. Sprinkle lightly with cinnamon-sugar and bake for 25 minutes in the preheated oven, or until golden brown.
* There should be 12 to 15 thin slices of unpeeled red apple for this recipe.

Tomato-Parmesan Corn Bread

Courtesy of The Florida Tomatoes
  Serves 8

With hearty stews, soups, or a big antipasto salad, this tomato-flecked corn bread is sure to please. Serve leftovers for breakfast halved, buttered, and grilled, topped with creamy scrambled eggs.

Ingredients:

1		large Florida tomato, cored and halved crosswise
4	tablespoons	unsalted butter
1	cup	yellow cornmeal
1	cup	unbleached all-purpose flour
½	cup	freshly grated parmesan cheese
1	tablespoon	sugar
2	teaspoons	baking powder
¼	teaspoon	baking soda
½	teaspoon	salt
1	teaspoon	dried oregano
1	teaspoon	dried basil
2		large eggs, slightly beaten
1	cup	milk
¼	cup	plain yogurt

Directions:

1. Using your finger, push the seeds and surrounding liquid out of the tomato. Dice the tomato and set it aside in a strainer to drain.
2. Gently melt the butter in a one inch cast-iron skillet and remove from the heat. Preheat the oven to 400F.
3. In a large bowl, mix the cornmeal, flour, cheese, sugar, baking powder, baking soda, salt, and herbs. In a separate bowl, blend the eggs, milk, and yogurt. Pour the melted butter into the liquid, but leave a heavy coating of butter in the pan.
4. Make a well in the dry mixture and add the liquid. Stir briskly to blend, then fold in the diced tomato. Turn the batter into the buttered skillet and bake for 25 minutes, until the surface is light golden. The top should resist gentle finger pressure. Let stand for five minutes, then slice and serve.

Extra-Cheesy Corn Bread

Serves 6

Ingredients:

1	cup	corn meal, white if possible
1	cup	unbleached flour
1	tablespoon	baking powder
1½	teaspoons	salt
10	ounces	cheddar, sharp, shredded
1	cup	milk
¼	cup	butter, melted
1		egg, large, beaten

Directions:

Combine the dry ingredients and then stir in the cheddar cheese. Combine the milk, butter, and egg. Then add them to the dry ingredients, mixing until just moistened. Pour into a greased 8-inch square baking pan and bake at 425F for 35 minutes. Serve hot.

Tomato Parmesan Corn Bread usually disappeared before dinner time.

Best Blueberry Muffins always guaranteed a big smile from the kids, and from pop.

Best Blueberry Muffins

Courtesy of The Wheat Foods Council
   Serves 12

Ingredients:

1		egg
¼	cup	oil
½	cup	milk
1½	cups	all-purpose flour
½	cup	sugar
2	teaspoons	baking powder
2	teaspoons	salt
1	cup	blueberries

Directions:

Grease bottoms of 2½ inch muffin or gem pan cups. Heat oven to 400F. Beat egg until foamy in a small mixing bowl. Beat in oil and then milk. In separate bowl, sift together dry ingredients. Stir blueberries into dry ingredients. Make a well in the center and pour in liquid ingredients. Stir quickly with fork just until dry ingredients are moistened. Batter will be lumpy. Using ¼ cup measure (not quite full) dip batter into muffin cups, filling each slightly more than half full. (Try to dip only once for each cup; muffins will be lighter.) Bake 18 to 20 minutes, or until golden and muffins test done with a tooth pick. Loosen with spatula and turn out. Best served warm. Note: Blueberries may be fresh, frozen, or canned (drain). Half whole wheat may be used for the flour if you enjoy a whole grain muffin.

Mom's Apricot Muffins

Serves 8

Ingredients:

½	cup	dried apricots, finely snipped
½	cup	unsweetened apple juice
1	cup	whole wheat flour
2	teaspoons	baking powder
¼	teaspoon	baking soda
¼	teaspoon	ground cardamom
¼	cup	walnuts, chopped
3	tablespoons	vegetable oil
1	tablespoon	sugar
1		egg

Directions:

Soak the apricots in the apple juice for 10 minutes. Combine the flour, baking powder, baking soda, cardamom, and walnuts in a bowl. Beat together the oil, sugar, and egg. Add the apricots, with the juice, and egg mixture to the flour. Mix just until all the ingredients are blended. Spoon into oiled muffin tins or paper muffin cups, filling ¾ full. Bake in a 350F oven for 10 to 15 minutes, or until golden brown.

Mom'n'Pop's
Soups, Stews and Chili

Creamy Cauliflower Soup

Serves 8

Ingredients:

1		cauliflower (about 2 pounds) separated into florets
2	cups	water
1	large	stalk celery, chopped (¾ cup)
1	medium	onion, chopped (½ cup)
1	tablespoon	lemon juice
2	tablespoons	margarine or butter
2	tablespoons	all-purpose flour
2½	cups	chicken broth
½	teaspoon	salt
¼	teaspoon	pepper
1	dash	nutmeg
½	cup	whipping (heavy) cream

Directions:

Heat 2 cups water to boiling in 3-quart saucepan. Add cauliflower florets and pieces, celery, onion, and lemon juice. Cover and heat to a boil, about 10 minutes or until cauliflower is tender (do not drain). Place in blender. Cover and blend until of uniform consistency. Heat margarine in 3-quart saucepan over medium heat until melted. Stir in flour. Cook, stirring constantly, until mixture is smooth and bubbly. Remove from heat. Stir in chicken broth. Heat to boiling, stirring constantly. Boil and stir 1 minute. Stir in cauliflower mixture, salt, pepper, and nutmeg. Heat just to boiling. Stir in whipping cream. Heat just until hot (do not boil). Serve with shredded cheese if desired.

Cold-Day Beef-Noodle Soup

Serves 6

Ingredients:

1	pound	ground beef
1	can	14 ounce Italian tomato sauce
8	cups	water
2		onions, chopped
1	pound	frozen corn, peas, carrots, mixed
6	ounces	egg noodles
1½	tablespoons	extra virgin olive oil
1	tablespoon	oregano
1	tablespoon	Mexican chili powder
1	tablespoon	freshly ground pepper
2	teaspoons	red cayenne pepper
2	teaspoons	salt

Directions:

Put 8 cups of water, one 14 ounce can of Italian tomato sauce, 2 medium sized onions (chopped), and 1 pound of mixed frozen vegetables into a pot. Add the seasoning and olive oil. Heat on high for 30 minutes. Brown the beef in a frying pan. Transfer the beef to the soup mixture, using a slotted spoon to leave the fat in the frying pan. Turn the heat to medium, heat for 10 minutes. Add the egg noodles. Turn the heat to low and heat another 20 minutes. Taste and adjust seasoning. Serve with grated parmesan cheese.

Mom's Best Potato Soup

Serves 8

Ingredients:

6	medium	potatoes, peeled and sliced
2		carrots, diced
6		celery stalks, diced
2	quarts	water
1		onion, chopped
6	tablespoons	butter or margarine
6	tablespoons	all-purpose flour
1	teaspoon	salt
½	teaspoon	pepper
1½	cups	milk

Directions:

In a large kettle, cook potatoes, carrots, and celery in water until tender, about 20 minutes. Drain, reserving liquid and setting vegetables aside. In the same kettle, sauté onion in butter until soft. Stir in flour, salt, and pepper. Gradually add milk, stirring constantly until thickened. Gently stir in cooked vegetables. Add 1 cup or more of reserved cooking liquid until soup is desired consistency.

Cream 'o' Potato Soup

Serves 4

Ingredients:

4	tablespoons	unsalted butter
2		onions, chopped
1		leek, white part only, thinly sliced
3		ribs celery, diced
4		waxy boiling potatoes, peeled and diced
1	teaspoon	sweet paprika
6	cups	chicken broth
½	teaspoon	dried thyme
1	small	bay leaf
5		sprigs parsley tied together with kitchen string
1	teaspoon	Worcestershire sauce
¾	cup	heavy cream
1	tablespoon	minced fresh parsley leaves

salt and freshly ground black pepper to taste

Directions:

Place the butter and onion in a large soup kettle, set over low heat and cook until onions have softened, about 5 minutes. Increase the heat to medium, add the leek and stir-cook 1 minute. Add the potatoes and paprika. Stir-cook 30 seconds. Stir in the broth, thyme, herb bundle, and worcestershire sauce. Bring the soup base to a boil, then cover and simmer 50 minutes or until the potatoes are tender. Scoop out about 1 cup of the vegetables and mash them. Then return them to the pot. Discard the herb bundle. (The soup may be prepared in advance up to this point.) Stir in the heavy cream, season with salt and pepper to taste, and let the soup cook without simmering until hot throughout. Sprinkle with fresh parsley if desired and serve immediately.

Old-Fashioned Pea Soup

Serves 6

Ingredients:

1	pound	dry, split green peas
8	cups	water
2		stalks celery, chopped (1 cup)
2	large	carrots coarsely chopped (1 cup)
1	medium	onion coarsely chopped (½ cup)
1	teaspoon	salt
1	teaspoon	dried thyme, crushed
½	teaspoon	pepper
¼	cup	snipped parsley
	or	
2	tablespoons	dried parsley flakes
4	cups	hot cooked brown rice

Directions:

In a dutch oven combine peas, water, celery, carrots, onion, salt, thyme, and pepper. Bring to boiling. Reduce heat. Simmer, covered, 45 to 60 minutes, or until peas are tender. Add parsley. Simmer, uncovered, 45 to 60 minutes, or until thick. Place ½ cup hot cooked brown rice on top of each serving.

Lima Bean Soup With Ham

Serves 4 to 6

Ingredients:

2	tablespoons	butter
12	ounces	red-skinned potatoes, cubed
1	cup	chopped onion
1	cup	mixture of green and red bell pepper
28	ounces	chicken broth
2	cups	milk
10	ounces	frozen lima beans
8	ounces	cooked smoked ham, cut up

Directions:

Melt butter in 5 quart pot over medium-high heat. Add potatoes, onion, and peppers. Cook about 8 minutes, until onion and peppers are tender. Stir in remaining ingredients, except ham. Bring to a boil. Reduce heat to medium. Add ham and simmer 10 to 15 minutes, until hot and lima beans are tender.

Veal and Barley Soup

Courtesy of The National Cattleman's Association
Serves 4

Ingredients:

1	pound	veal for stew, cut into 1 inch pieces
5	teaspoons	vegetable oil, divided
1	teaspoon	salt
¼	teaspoon	coarse grind black pepper
1		medium onion, coarsely chopped
5	cups	water
½	cup	medium pearled barley
2	medium	chopped carrots
1	teaspoon	Italian seasoning, crushed
1	cup	short, thin fresh spinach strips, lightly packed

Directions:

Heat 2 teaspoons oil in dutch oven or large, deep saucepan over medium heat. Brown veal for stew (½ at a time), using additional 2 teaspoons oil as needed. Remove veal from pan; season with salt and pepper. Reserve. Heat remaining 1 teaspoon oil in same pan over medium heat. Add onion; cook for five minutes or until tender, stirring occasionally. Return reserved veal to pan. Stir in water, barley, carrots, and Italian seasoning. Bring to a boil; reduce heat to low. Cover and simmer 45 minutes, or until veal and barley are tender. Stir in spinach; heat through.

Veal and Barley Soup was perfect on those really cold days.

Deluxe Cream of Tomato Soup

Courtesy of The Florida Tomatoes
Serves 4 to 6

This soup has the real thing: fresh tomatoes and heavy cream, and you can taste the difference. On top of that, it's a real breeze to prepare. Round it out with grilled cheese sandwiches, potato chips, and pickles, and you've got the makings for a surefire family favorite.

Ingredients:

1		small onion, finely chopped
2		celery ribs, finely chopped
4		large Florida tomatoes, peeled, cored, seeded, and chopped (see note)
1	teaspoon	sugar
2	cups	chicken broth
½	cup	heavy cream
2	tablespoons	unsalted butter
2	teaspoons	chopped fresh dill or
1	teaspoon	dried dill weed

salt and freshly ground pepper to taste

Deluxe Cream of Tomato Soup warms the tummy.

Directions:
1. Melt the butter in a medium-size saucepan. Add the onion and celery and sauté gently over medium heat for five minutes, stirring often; do not brown. Stir in the tomatoes and sugar. Simmer, covered, for 6 to 8 minutes, until the tomatoes are soft.
2. Transfer the vegetables to a food processor and process to a smooth puree. Pour the puree back into the saucepan and stir in the remaining ingredients. Heat the soup through, correcting the seasoning. Serve hot.
Note: To peel the tomatoes, submerge them for 15 to 30 seconds in boiling water. Remove to a colander and rinse briefly under cold water. The skins will slip right off.

Mom's Own Chicken Soup

Serves 6

Ingredients:

1	tablespoon	canola oil
1	cup	onion, finely diced
½	cup	celery, finely diced
1		cinnamon stick
12		whole black peppercorns
1¾	pounds	chicken breasts (3½ ounces per serving, skinned, with all fat removed and cut into pieces

3	teaspoons	garlic, minced
3	teaspoons	ginger root, minced
¼	teaspoon	salt (optional)
¼	teaspoon	ground turmeric
2	cups	tomatoes, fresh or canned, without salt, blended
6	cups	water
½	pound	potatoes, peeled and cut into 12 pieces
½	cup	parsley, chopped
2	tablespoons	lemon juice

Directions:
1. In a saucepan, heat oil and sauté onions, celery, cinnamon, and peppercorns until onions and celery are soft. Do not let onions brown.
2. Add chicken, garlic, ginger, salt if desired, turmeric, and tomatoes. Mix well, cover, and cook for 15 minutes. Stir occasionally.
3. Add 6 cups of water, potatoes and parsley. Mix well, cover, and cook for 15 minutes, or until the potatoes are done.
4. Add lemon juice, mix and serve.

Hearty Beef Stew and Dumplings

Courtesy of The National Cattleman's Beef Association
Serves 24 (48 dumplings)

Ingredients:

½	cup	vegetable oil
6	pounds	beef for stewing, cubed 1 inch
6	ounces	flour
2	tablespoons	dried thyme leaves
8		bay leaves
1	tablespoon	black pepper
2	teaspoons	salt
18	cups	beef broth
1½	cups	(12 fluid ounces) dry red wine
3	ounces	beef base (condensed, similar to bullion)
3	tablespoons	(1½ fluid ounces) browning and seasoning sauce
2	pounds	(4 ounces) carrots, cut 1 inch
2	pounds	(4 ounces) onions, cut 1 inch
2	pounds	(4 ounces) potatoes, not peeled, cut 1 inch
1	pound	(5 ounces) celery, cut 1 inch
2	pounds	(4 ounces) frozen peas, thawed

parsley, fresh, chopped, as needed

Directions:

1. Heat oil in large braising pan over medium-high heat. Add beef; sauté, stirring occasionally, until browned on all sides.
2. Sprinkle seasonings over beef; cook, stirring, 4 minutes.
3. Add vegetables; bring to boil. Reduce heat; cover and simmer, stirring occasionally, 30 to 45 minutes, or until vegetables are tender and gravy is slightly thickened. Remove bay leaves. Keep hot.
4. For each serving: Portion 1½ cups beef stew into individual ovenproof au gratin dish; stir in 1½ ounces peas. Top with 2 dumplings. Cover with aluminum foil; heat in 400F oven about 10 minutes or until hot.
5. Garnish with parsley before serving.

Directions:

Dumplings: Combine 2 pounds, 6 ounces buttermilk baking mix and 2 cups (16 fluid ounces) milk in large bowl. Portion into forty-eight 1½ ounce dumplings. Steam dumplings on greased, inverted, perforated pan about 10 minutes, or until cooked through. Remove from pan; cover and reserve. Makes 48 dumplings.

Turkey Stew 'n' Dumplings

Serves 4 to 5

Ingredients:

1¼	pounds	turkey breast tenderloins
4		slices diced bacon
4		carrots cut in chunks
2		quartered onions
2		stalks celery, cut in chunks
2	cups	water, divided
¼	teaspoon	rosemary
1		bay leaf
3	tablespoons	flour
1	cup	all-purpose baking mix
½	cup	milk
4	ounce	can chicken broth

salt and pepper to taste

Directions:

Sauté bacon in dutch oven until partially crisp. Cut turkey into 1 inch chunks and add with onion. Sauté until meat is no longer pink. Add carrots, celery, 1¾ cup water, broth, rosemary, and bay leaf. Bring to a boil. Reduce heat, cover, and simmer for 20 minutes. Mix flour with ¼ cup of water and stir into stew mixture. Bring to boil, stirring constantly. Remove bay leaf. Salt and pepper to taste. Add baking mix and milk and drop by rounded tablespoons onto stew. Cook uncovered for 10 minutes. Cover and cook 10 minutes longer.

Home-Made Chicken Stew

Serves 6

Ingredients:

1		1½ to 2 pound stewing chicken, cut up
1	tablespoon	vegetable oil or shortening
3	cups	hot water
½	teaspoon	salt
¼	teaspoon	pepper
2	medium	carrots, cut into 1 inch pieces
1	large	potato, cut into 1½ inch pieces (about 1¼ cups)
1	medium	turnip, cut into 1 inch pieces (about 1 cup)
1	medium	stalk celery, cut into 1 inch pieces (about 1 cup)
1	small	onion, chopped (about ¼ cup)
½	teaspoon	browning sauce, if desired
1	teaspoon	salt
1		bay leaf
½	cup	cold water
2	tablespoons	all-purpose flour

(Dumplings can be added to the stew if desired)

Pop often liked to peek in the kitchen to "check on how dinner was coming," and mom didn't mind.

Directions:

Cook and stir chicken in oil in 12-inch skillet or dutch oven about 15 minutes or until chicken is brown. Add 3 cups hot water, ½ teaspoon salt, and the pepper. Heat to boiling, reduce heat. Cover and simmer 2 to 2½ hours or until chicken is almost tender. Stir in carrots, potato, turnip, bell pepper, celery, onion, browning sauce, 1 teaspoon salt, and the bay leaf. Cover and simmer about 30 minutes, or until vegetables are tender. Remove bay leaf. Prepare parsley dumplings. Shake ½ cup cold water and the flour in tightly covered container. Gradually stir into stew. Heat to boiling, stirring constantly. Boil and stir 1 minute. Reduce heat. If using dumplings add them now. Drop dumpling dough by 10 to 12 spoonfuls onto hot stew (do not drop directly into liquid). Cook uncovered 10 minutes. Cover and cook 10 minutes longer.

Old-Fashioned Bean Soup

Serves 6

Ingredients:

1	pound	navy beans
1	pound	beef stew meat
1	pound	prunes
1		sliced onion
1	quart	cut carrots
		salt and pepper
1½	quarts	cut potatoes
12		whole cloves

Directions:

Soak 1 pound navy beans overnight. Cook beans, prunes, beef and vegetables separately. Do not drain. Mix and simmer until the flavors are blended.

Burgundy Beef Stew

Courtesy of The National Cattleman's Beef Association
Serves 4

Ingredients:

1	pound	boneless beef chuck
3	tablespoons	all-purpose flour, divided
1	teaspoon	salt
¼	teaspoon	pepper
1	tablespoon	vegetable oil
4	medium	carrots, sliced ½ inch thick
8	small	onions
½	cup	red wine
1	tablespoon	ketchup
1	clove	garlic, crushed
¼	teaspoon	dried marjoram leaves, crushed
¼	teaspoon	dried thyme leaves, crushed
4	ounces	mushrooms, halved
2	tablespoons	water
2	tablespoons	chopped fresh parsley

Directions:
Trim excess fat from beef chuck; cut beef into 1½ inch cubes. Combine 2 tablespoons flour, salt, and pepper; dredge beef. Place beef and oil in 11 x 7½ inch microwave safe baking dish. Cover and microwave at medium low, or 30 percent power, 20 minutes, stirring after 10 minutes. Add carrots and onions. Combine wine, ketchup, garlic, marjoram and thyme. Pour over beef and vegetables, stirring to combine. Cover and continue to microwave at medium low for 45 minutes, stirring every 15 minutes. Add mushrooms and continue to microwave at medium low, 15 to 25 minutes, or until beef and vegetables are tender. Combine remaining 1 tablespoon flour and water; stir into beef and vegetables. Sprinkle with parsley. Cover and microwave at medium low for 3 minutes, stirring after 1½ minutes.

Burgundy Beef Stew was for those special nights when mom 'n' pop dined alone.

Lamb Vegetable Soup was always a big favorite.

Beef Barley Soup

Serves 10 to 12

Ingredients:

1	tablespoon	cooking oil
2	pounds	short ribs
2	medium	onions, chopped
3		carrots, sliced
3	stalks	celery, sliced
1	28 ounce can	whole tomatoes, chopped
2	teaspoons	water
4	cubes	chicken bouillon
½	cup	medium pearl barley

Lamb Vegetable Soup

Courtesy of The American Lamb Council
Serves 6-8

Ingredients:

2	pounds	cubed lamb, trimmed of all fat (bones may be added for flavor, if desired)
2	quarts	water
1	tablespoon	salt
4	whole cloves	garlic
4	whole	peppercorns
1		large onion, chopped
1		turnip, chopped
¼	cup	barley or rice
2	cups	chopped fresh or canned tomatoes
3	cups	frozen mixed vegetables or vegetables of choice
1	tablespoon	dried parsley leaves

Directions:
Place lamb, water, salt, cloves, peppercorns, onion, turnip, barley or rice, tomatoes, vegetables, and parsley in electric slow cooker. Cover. Cook on low for about 10 hours. Flavorful additions to lamb vegetable soup: zucchini, yellow squash, okra, spinach, cabbage. Add ½ teaspoon ground oregano, summer savory, or sweet basil.

Directions:
In a large dutch oven or kettle, heat oil over medium-high. Brown beef. Add onions, carrots, celery, tomatoes, water, and bouillon. Bring to a boil. Cover and simmer for about 2 hours, or until beef is tender. Add barley. Simmer another 50-60 minutes, or until barley is done.

Grandma's Best Bean Stew

Serves 4

Ingredients:

½	cup	olive oil
2		onions, chopped
4		garlic cloves
2	pounds	runner beans, trimmed and sliced
1	pound	tomatoes, chopped
1	tablespoon	sugar
1	teaspoon	salt
½	teaspoon	black pepper
2	cups	stock

Directions:
Heat oil in a pot and fry the onion for 2 minutes. Add garlic and fry together. Add the rest of the ingredients and the seasonings. Mix together well. Fry for 5 minutes. Add stock. Simmer until the beans are tender. Serve hot or cold.

Classic Chicken Gumbo

Courtesy of The National Broiler Council
Serves 6

Ingredients:

1		broiler-fryer chicken, cooked, skinned, boned and cut into bite-size pieces
2	tablespoons	shortening
2	tablespoons	flour
2		onions, finely chopped
1		green pepper, finely chopped
6	cups	warm chicken broth
8		tomatoes, peeled and chopped
½	pound	okra, cut in ¼ inch pieces
½	cup	long grain rice, uncooked
2		ribs celery, chopped
1	teaspoon	salt
½	teaspoon	pepper
½	teaspoon	fresh thyme leaves
1		bay leaf
1	teaspoon	file powder (powdered young leaves of sassafras)

Directions:

In large dutch oven, heat shortening at a low temperature. Add flour and stir until brown, about 15 minutes. (Do not hurry; if flour burns, roux is ruined). Add onion and green pepper and cook until onion is transparent, about 5 minutes. Slowly add warm broth and stir until broth boils. Add tomatoes, okra, rice, celery, salt, pepper, thyme leaves, and bay leaf; bring to a boil, add chicken. When mixture boils again, reduce heat to low, cover, and cook about 20 minutes. Stir, cover again and cook 20 minutes more. Remove from heat and add file powder (Do not boil after adding file powder).

Corn Chowder

Serves 4

Ingredients:

1	medium	potato, diced
1		onion, chopped
1	can	(14 ounce) chicken broth
1	can	(16 ounce) cream-style corn
2	cups	milk
2	tablespoons	butter
1		egg, slightly beaten
1	can	(8 ounce) corn

Directions:

Sauté onion in butter until golden brown. Add broth and potato and simmer until potato is tender. Add corn and milk. Blend well. Season with salt and pepper. Bring to a boil. Remove from heat. Stir some of chowder into egg. Add mixture to sauce pan and blend well. Simmer until heated through. Serve hot.

Mom's Corn Chowder

Serves 8

Ingredients:

1	medium	onion, chopped
3	medium	potatoes, diced
2	medium	carrots, sliced
1	large	celery stalk, chopped
2		bay leaves
2	tablespoons	vegetable oil
3	cups	corn
1	can	(14 ounces) tomatoes, chopped
1½	teaspoon	coriander
1	teaspoon	savory
½	teaspoon	thyme
1	cup	water
1½	cup	chicken stock
		salt and pepper to taste

Directions:

Place onions, potatoes, carrots, celery, bay leaves, and oil in a large soup pot and add just enough stock to cover. Bring to a boil and simmer over low heat for 10 minutes. Add the corn and the tomatoes with their liquid and simmer for 10 minutes. Add the seasonings and simmer for another 10 minutes. Remove ¾ cup of potatoes and mash well. Return to the pot with the 1 cup of stock. Stir well. Simmer for another 5 minutes, or until you are ready to serve it.

Pop's Turkey-Macaroni Chili

Serves 8

Ingredients:

2	tablespoons	cooking oil
1	package	fresh ground turkey
1		onion, medium, chopped
2½	cups	chicken broth
1	package	(7 ounce) elbow macaroni, uncooked
1	can	(15 ounce) tomato sauce
1	tablespoon	vinegar
1½	teaspoons	sugar
1	teaspoon	chili powder
1	teaspoon	garlic salt
¼	cup	grated parmesan cheese
2	tablespoons	grated parmesan cheese
1	tablespoon	parsley

Directions:
Heat oil in 4 quart dutch oven over medium-high heat until hot. Crumble turkey into dutch oven and stir in onion. Cook until turkey is no longer pink. Drain, reserving juices in dutch oven. Stir broth into juices. Heat to boiling. Stir in macaroni. Reduce heat and simmer, stirring frequently, until broth is almost absorbed, about 10 minutes. Stir in turkey mixture and remaining ingredients, except 2 tablespoons of cheese. Cook over low heat 10 minutes. Salt and pepper to taste. Sprinkle the rest of the cheese on top of each portion and serve.

Old-Fashioned Chili

Serves 4

Ingredients:

8	ounces	dried black-eyed peas
1	pound	sausage meat
3	can	tomatoes
2	cups	water
1	tablespoon	black pepper
2	tablespoons	garlic salt
2	tablespoons	chili powder

Directions:
Cover the black-eyed peas in water and soak overnight. Drain peas. Sauté sausage meat until done. Add tomatoes, water, and all spices. Simmer one hour.

Quick 'n' Easy Chili

Serves 6

Ingredients:

1½	pounds	beef, chicken, or turkey
2	cups	water
1	tablespoon	chili powder
1	tablespoon	curry powder
3		tomatoes, diced
4	cups	cooked kidney beans
1		onion, chopped
1		bunch green onions, sliced
1½	cups	grated natural sharp cheese

Directions:
In a frying pan, sauté meat until lightly browned. Pour off drippings. Add water, chili, and curry powder. Simmer 5 minutes. Add tomatoes and beans. Heat through. Stir in onions. Ladle into serving bowls and sprinkle cheese on top.

Mom's Chili with Chicken

Serves 8

Ingredients:

1	pound	skinned and boned chicken breasts cut into 1 inch cubes
2	tablespoons	corn oil
4	medium	onions, chopped
2	large	green peppers, coarsely chopped (optional)
3	large cloves	garlic, minced
1	teaspoon	cumin
1	teaspoon	oregano
½	teaspoon	thyme
		salt
		pepper
2		bay leaves
3	tablespoons	chili powder
3	cans	undrained tomatoes (1 pound each)
1	cup	plain low fat yogurt
¼	cup	minced fresh parsley
1		lemon
1	can	tomato paste

Directions:
Wrap chicken and freeze until firm, but not solid. Grind coarsely in processor, using on/off turns. Heat oil in large dutch oven over medium-high heat. Add onions, green peppers, and garlic and cook until golden brown, stirring frequently, about 15 minutes. Mix in cumin, oregano, coriander, and thyme and stir for 2 minutes. Add chicken and bay leaves. Cook about 5 minutes. Add chili powder.
Reduce heat to medium and cook 5 minutes, stirring frequently. Add tomatoes, breaking up large pieces with a spoon. Mix in tomato paste, salt, and pepper. Reduce heat, cover, and simmer 45 minutes, stirring occasionally.
Uncover, reduce heat to lowest setting, and cook 1½ hours, stirring frequently near end and adding water if necessary to prevent burning. Adjust seasoning.
(Can be prepared 1 day ahead and refrigerated.) Sprinkle avocado with lemon juice. Ladle chili into large soup bowls. Spoon 2 teaspoons of yogurt in center of each. Top with parsley. Serve hot.

New Basic Beef Chili

Courtesy of The National Cattleman's Beef Association
Serves 120 (if each portion size equals 1 cup of the
    beef mixture)

Ingredients:

13¾	pounds	ground beef, 80 percent lean
1½	gallons	hot tap water
4	no. 10 cans	whole tomatoes, canned, not drained
3	no. 10 cans	kidney beans, canned, not drained
½	no. 10 can	tomato paste
8	ounces	bulgur
6	ounces	low-sodium beef base
4	ounces	onions, minced, dehydrated
¾	cup	chili powder
6	tablespoons	sugar
3¾	pounds	part-skim mozzarella cheese shredded optional)
2	pounds	corn chips (optional)

Directions:

1. Place ground beef in steam kettle. Cook ground beef. While cooking, use kettle whip to break beef into crumbles, about ¼ to ½ inch pieces. Cook until no longer pink. Turn off heat. Drain fat from cooked beef. While draining, stir beef by pulling kettle whip through beef in a circular motion, and then zig-zag-stir through all sections of beef.

2. Add enough hot tap water to just cover beef. Stir beef and water by pulling kettle whip through beef in a circular motion, and then zig-zag-stir through all sections of beef. Drain fat and liquid from cooked beef. While draining, stir beef and water by pulling kettle whip through beef in a circular motion, and then zig-zag-stir through all sections of beef.

3. Grind tomatoes; add to rinsed beef in steam kettle.

4. Add remaining ingredients; mix well. Simmer for 1 hour, stirring occasionally.

5. For each serving: Portion 1 cup hot chili. Garnish with ½ ounce shredded cheese and ¼ ounce corn chips, if desired.

New Basic Beef Chili recalls the wonderful chili we used to have over at grandma's house.

Chili for Kids is a great meal that you can make in one of those new microwave ovens.

Chili For Kids

Courtesy of The National Cattleman's Beef Association
  Serves 4

Ingredients:

1	pound	ground beef (80 percent lean)
½	cup	chopped onion
¼	teaspoon	garlic powder
1	tablespoon	chili powder
1	teaspoon	ground cumin
½	teaspoon	salt
1	dash	hot pepper sauce, if desired
1	can	(28 ounces) peeled whole tomatoes, not drained and coarsely chopped
1	can	(8 ounces) kidney beans, drained shredded cheese

Add to taste: ripe olives and dairy sour cream

Directions:
Combine ground beef, onion, and garlic powder; arrange in a ring in microwave-safe sieve or small colander. Place sieve in microwave-safe bowl. Microwave at high 6 minutes, stirring to break up beef after 3 minutes. Stir beef after removing from oven. Pour off drippings. Place beef in 2 quart microwave-safe dish; sprinkle chili powder, cumin, salt, and pepper sauce, if desired, over beef, stirring to combine. Stir in tomatoes and kidney beans. Cover with waxed paper and microwave at high for 12 to 14 minutes, stirring every 4 minutes. Serve with shredded cheese, ripe olives and sour cream as desired.
Note: Recipe was tested in 650-watt microwave oven. If your oven has a different wattage adjust times accordingly.

Mom'n'Pop's
Potato and Vegetable Side Dishes

Mom's Scalloped Potatoes

Serves 8

Ingredients:

6	cups	potatoes, raw, sliced thin
3	tablespoons	butter
3	tablespoons	flour
1½	cups	milk
1	teaspoon	salt
1	teaspoon	cayenne
1	cup	processed cheese, grated
½	cups	chopped pimento

Directions:

For sauce: In a saucepan, melt butter. Then blend in flour. Cook over moderate heat and slowly stir in milk. Season with salt and cayenne. Continue cooking until sauce is smooth and boiling. Reduce heat and add cheese, stirring, until cheese is blended. Add the pimento mixture, stir, and remove from heat. Grease a baking dish and fill with alternate layers of potatoes and sauce. Bake in moderate oven, 350F, until potatoes are done, about 1½ to 2 hours. Potatoes may be turned with a spoon to ensure even cooking.

Baked Tomatoes with Corn

Serves 6

Ingredients:

1	can	(16 ounce) tomatoes
1	tablespoon	sugar
	pinch	rosemary
	pinch	black pepper
16	ounces	frozen corn kernels
2		onions, chopped
2	tablespoons	hot sauce
1	tablespoon	margarine
½	teaspoon	salt
2	cups	dry, lightly crushed potato chips
1	cup	grated cheese

Directions:

Pour off the liquid from the canned tomatoes. Simmer the tomatoes with the sugar and spices for about 5 minutes. Add the corn and onion, hot sauce, margarine, and salt. Cook slowly for about 15 minutes. Spray a casserole dish with nonstick vegetable spray. Place alternate layers of vegetable mixture, lightly crushed potato chips, and cheese, ending up with a layer of cheese. Bake in a 400F oven for about 20 minutes, or until the top is brown.

Around our house, you could always tell when the potatoes came out of the oven.

Grandma's Special Old-Fashioned Succotash

Serves 6

Ingredients:

3	pounds	lima beans*
4		stalks of corn*
3	slices	bacon, cut up
1	small	onion, chopped (about ¼ cup)
½	cup	half and half
¼	teaspoon	salt
¼	teaspoon	pepper

Directions:
Prepare lima beans as directed. Prepare corn as directed. Cut enough kernels from corn cobs to measure 2 cups. Reserve. Heat beans, bacon, onion, and enough water to cover. Bring to a boil in a 3 quart saucepan. Reduce heat. Cover and simmer 20 to 25 minutes, or until beans are tender. Stir in corn. Heat to boiling. Reduce heat. Cover and simmer 5 minutes, or until corn is tender. Drain. Stir in half and half, salt, and pepper. Heat, stirring occasionally, until hot.
*Substitute: 2 packs (9 ounces of each) frozen lima beans and 2 cups of corn. When substituting frozen vegetables, heat beans, bacon, onion, and enough water to cover. Bring to a boil in a 3 quart saucepan. Reduce heat. Cover and simmer 5 minutes. Stir in corn. Heat to boiling, and then reduce heat. Cover and simmer about 3 minutes, or until beans and corn are tender. Continue as directed.

Pop's Ham Potatoes with Cheese

Serves 2

Ingredients:

2	cups	sliced, peeled potatoes, cooked
1	cup	diced cooked ham
1	tablespoon	minced onion
¼	cup	butter or margarine
3	tablespoons	all-purpose flour
1½	cups	milk
1	cup	shredded cheddar cheese (4 ounces)
¾	teaspoon	salt
1	dash	white pepper chopped fresh parsley

Directions:
Combine potatoes, ham, and onion in a greased 1 quart casserole. Set aside. In a saucepan, melt butter over medium heat. Stir in flour until smooth. Gradually add milk, stirring constantly until mixture thickens and bubbles. Add cheese, salt and pepper. Stir until the cheese melts. Pour over potato mixture and stir gently to mix. Bake at 350F for 35-40 minutes, or until bubbly. Garnish with parsley.

Mom's Orange-Glazed Sweet Potatoes

Serves 4

Ingredients:

6	medium	sweet potatoes or yams (about 2 pounds)*
½	cup	packed brown sugar
3	tablespoons	margarine or butter
3	tablespoons	orange juice
½	teaspoon	salt
1	tablespoon	grated orange peel

Directions:
Prepare and cook sweet potatoes. Slip off skins. Cut into ½ inch slices. Heat remaining ingredients in 10 inch skillet over medium heat, stirring constantly, until smooth and bubbly. Add sweet potatoes. Stir gently until glazed and hot.
*Substitute: 1 can (23 ounces) sweet potatoes or Yams, drained and cut into slices.

Grandma's Easy Scalloped Potatoes

Serves 6

Ingredients:

2	pounds	potatoes, peeled, sliced
½	cup	chopped onion
3	tablespoons	all-purpose flour
½	teaspoon	salt
¼	teaspoon	pepper
1	tablespoon	low fat margarine
3	cups	skimmed milk, heated
vegetable spray		

Directions:
Preheat oven to 400F. Lightly spray a 2 quart casserole with vegetable spray. Arrange a layer of potatoes in casserole, then sprinkle with some of onion, flour, salt and pepper.
Continue to layer until all potatoes, onion, flour, salt and pepper are used. Dot top with margarine. Then pour milk over all. Bake 20 minutes. Then reduce heat to 350F and bake 50 to 60 minutes longer, or until tender.

Mom's Creamed Spinach

Serves 6

Ingredients:

¼	cup	spinach
1	dash	pepper
1	tablespoon	butter
¾	cup	milk
½	teaspoon	salt
¼	teaspoon	nutmeg
2	teaspoons	flour

Directions:

Pick over and wash spinach thoroughly. Add salt and cook until tender. Do not add water. Chop the spinach very fine. Melt the butter in a saucepan. Add the flour and blend. Slowly add the milk and stir constantly until mixture thickens. Combine with the chopped spinach. Add the pepper and nutmeg and serve.

Mom always kept the fridge well stocked.

Mom's Creamed Onions

Serves 4

Ingredients:

8		white onions
½	pint	whipping cream
4	tablespoons	flour
¼	teaspoon	cayenne pepper
4	tablespoons	butter
½	teaspoon	salt

Directions:

Peel the onions. Parboil in about ¾ cup water. Make white sauce with rest of ingredients. If you like a stronger onion flavor, thin the white sauce with part or all of the onion water. Otherwise, thin it with your choice of cream, milk, water, chicken broth, or another flavor if you wish. Add onions and bake at 325F to 350F until bubbly.

Home-Style Glazed Carrots

Serves 4

Ingredients:

6	medium	carrots, peeled and thinly sliced
3	tablespoons	dark brown sugar, firmly packed
3	tablespoons	butter or margarine
3	tablespoons	orange juice
1	teaspoon	lemon peel
¼	teaspoon	salt

Directions:

1. Combine all ingredients in a deep, 1-quart, heat-resistant, nonmetallic casserole.
2. Heat, covered, in microwave oven for 6 to 8 minutes, or until carrots are tender. Stir occasionally so that carrots are well glazed.

Easy Stewed Tomatoes

Serves 4

Ingredients:

1		(16-ounce) can whole tomatoes
½	tablespoon	butter
½	teaspoon	salt
½	teaspoon	sugar
1	tablespoon	cornstarch
1	tablespoon	diced celery
1	tablespoon	diced onion

Directions:

Bring all ingredients to a boil. Reduce heat and simmer for 10 minutes, or until mixture is of medium thickness.

Tomato and Garlic Baked Stuffed Potatoes were a big favorite at our house.

Tomato and Garlic Baked Stuffed Potatoes

Courtesy of The Florida Tomatoes
  Serves 6

Garlicky tomato chunks add a fresh new twist to an old favorite, baked stuffed potatoes.
To make these extra-generous, bake two extra potatoes and use their insides in the stuffing.

Ingredients:

8	extra-large	baking potatoes, scrubbed
1	tablespoon	olive oil
2	tablespoons	unsalted butter
1	large	onion, chopped
6	cloves	garlic, minced
2	large	fresh Florida tomatoes, cored, seeded, cut into bite-size chunks
1	tablespoon	red wine vinegar
½	cup	sour cream
½	cup	freshly grated parmesan cheese

salt and freshly ground pepper to taste

Directions:
1. Bake the potatoes until the flesh is tender. Slice the potatoes lengthwise and cool briefly. When they're cool enough to handle, spoon the flesh into a bowl, leaving a thick enough casing to support the filling. Reserve the 6 best casings.
2. Heat the olive oil and butter in a medium-size skillet. Add the onion and sauté over medium heat, stirring, for 10 to 12 minutes, until the onion is golden brown. Stir in the garlic, sauté for another minute, then remove from the heat and scrape into a bowl.
3. Put the skillet back on the heat. Add the tomatoes and sauté them for 1 to 2 minutes over medium heat, just until they start to soften. Stir in the vinegar, cook for a few more seconds, then transfer to the bowl with the onions. Preheat the oven to 400F.
4. Using a potato masher, mash the potato flesh with the sour cream, leaving it a little on the chunky side. Add the parmesan cheese, then fold in the reserved tomato mixture. Salt and pepper the stuffing to taste, then pack it into the reserved skins, dividing it equally.
5. Bake the potatoes for about 25 to 30 minutes, until heated through. Serve hot.

Mom'n'Pop's
Hot Dishes and Casseroles

Mom's Favorite Tuna Noodle Casserole

Serves 4

Ingredients:

4	ounces	medium sized noodles
1	tablespoon	margarine
10	ounce	package, frozen cut green beans
1	cup	chopped onion
¼	cup	sliced celery
1		garlic clove, minced
1½	cups	skim milk
½	cup	shredded Swiss cheese
1	can	(9¼ ounce can) tuna in water
1	cup	sliced mushrooms
1	teaspoon	chicken bouillon granules
½	teaspoon	dried dillweed
1	tablespoon	cornstarch
¼	cup	mayonnaise
1	cup	lightly crushed potato chips

Directions:

Cook noodles according to the directions on the package. Drain and set aside. Meanwhile, drain and flake tuna. Set aside. Melt margarine, then toss with lightly crushed potato chips. Set aside. In a large saucepan combine frozen green beans, mushrooms, onion, celery, bouillon granules, garlic, dillweed, and ½ cup water. Bring to boiling. Reduce heat. Cover. Simmer for 5 minutes, or until vegetables are tender. Meanwhile, stir together skim milk and cornstarch. Stir into vegetable mixture. Cook and stir until slightly thickened and bubbly. Remove from heat. Then stir in cheese and mayonnaise. Stir in noodles and tuna. Spoon mixture into a 2 quart casserole dish.

Sprinkle potato chip mixture over a casserole dish. Bake, uncovered, in a 350F oven for 25-30 minutes, or until crumbs are golden.

Grandma's Old-Fashioned Tuna Noodle Casserole

Serves 6

Ingredients:

6	ounces	egg noodles, medium sized
2	tablespoons	butter
1	can	cream of mushroom soup
1	cup	milk
½	cup	sour cream
½	teaspoon	salt
½	cup	onion, finely chopped
¼	cup	pimento, sliced
1	cup	celery, chopped
6½	ounces	tuna, drained and flaked
15		round snack crackers, broken but not crumbled
		parsley, for garnish

Directions:

Cook noodles in salted water. Drain. Coat with butter. Preheat your oven to 425F. In a large saucepan, mix soup, milk, sour cream, salt, onion, pimento, and celery. Cook over low heat, stirring frequently, for 15 minutes. Add tuna. Combine with noodles and pour into 2-quart casserole dish. Sprinkle top with crackers. Bake 20 to 25 minutes. Garnish with parsley before serving.

Quick 'n' Easy Tuna Dish

Serves 4

Ingredients:

1		envelope onion soup mix
10	ounces	frozen peas and carrots
6½	ounces	tuna, drained and flaked
1½	cups	milk
8	ounces	medium sized egg noodles
2	ounces	shredded cheddar cheese

Directions:
Preheat your oven to 350F, cook the noodles, and thaw the peas and carrots. In large bowl, blend onion soup mix with milk. Stir in peas and carrots, cooked noodles, and tuna. Place in greased 2-quart oblong baking dish. Then top with cheese. Bake 20 minutes, or until bubbling.

Easy Macaroni 'n' Cheese Bake

Serves 4 to 6

Ingredients:

1		small box elbow macaroni
3	cups	cheddar cheese, shredded
1	can	evaporated milk
1½	cups	homogenized milk
3		eggs
½		stick butter
		salt and pepper to taste

Directions:
Cook macaroni according to directions on box. Grease crock pot with butter. Mix all ingredients in crock pot. Cook on high for 30 minutes. Then turn to low and cook for 2 hours.

Pop's Favorite Macaroni 'n' Cheese

Serves 4

Ingredients:

½	pound	macaroni
1	cup	white sauce
1	teaspoon	prepared mustard
1	pinch	cayenne pepper
½	pound	sharp cheddar cheese, shredded
2	ounces	munster cheese, thin sliced
¼	cup	freshly ground parmesan cheese
2	tablespoons	lightly crushed potato chips
1	tablespoon	butter, cut in small pieces

salt and fresh ground pepper to taste

Directions:
Cook the macaroni in plenty of salted water until tender, 8 to 10 minutes. Drain and cool under cold running water. Prepare the white sauce, and while still hot, toss all but two tablespoons of it with the macaroni, mustard, cayenne, cheddar, salt, and pepper. Place in a large buttered casserole dish and top with the munster cheese. Bake in a preheated 375F oven for 15 minutes, or until the top is crusty and brown. Spread the remaining 2 tablespoons of white sauce over the top. Cover with a layer of parmesan cheese mixed with the lightly crushed potato chips. Dab with the butter. Return to the oven for 10 more minutes. Place under high broiler for 1 minute to brown the top and serve immediately. Makes 4 servings.

Mozzarella-Style Macaroni 'n' Cheese

Serves 4

Ingredients:

8	ounces	elbow macaroni
8	ounces	processed cheese
12	ounces	shredded mozzarella cheese
1	cup	sour cream
8	ounces	cream cheese
12	ounces	evaporated milk
½		stick butter

Directions:
Cook and drain macaroni. Place in ovenproof casserole dish. In a saucepan, melt processed cheese, sour cream, and cream cheese in the butter. Add evaporated milk. Stir until smooth. Add ¼ of the mozzarella. Pour over macaroni. Sprinkle remaining mozzarella over top. Bake at 375F for 30 minutes, or until bubbly. If it browns on top, the mozzarella will not be stringy.

Canned Ham Hot Dish

Serves 6 to 8

Ingredients:

1		7 ounce package elbow macaroni
2	tablespoons	margarine or butter
½	cup	chopped onion
1	cup	frozen peas and carrots
¼	teaspoons	pepper
2	cups	milk
1	cup	shredded Swiss cheese
1	can	(12 ounce) ham, cubed
2	tablespoons	flour
1	teaspoon	Dijon mustard
		buttered bread crumbs

Directions:
Prepare elbow macaroni according to package directions. Drain. In medium saucepan, melt margarine or butter. Add onion. Cook until tender. Stir in flour, mustard, and pepper. Blend in milk. Cook, stirring constantly, until thickened and bubbly. Add cheese. Stir until melted. Combine macaroni, ham, peas and carrots, and cheese sauce. Pour into a 3-quart baking dish. Top with bread crumbs. Bake in 350F oven until hot and bubbly, about 30 minutes.

Pop's Fool-Proof, Quick 'n' Easy Casserole

Serves 6

Ingredients:

1	pound	lean ground beef
½	cup	chopped onion (1 medium)
8	ounces	undrained whole kernel corn
1	can	8 ounces tomato sauce
¼	cup	1 can ripe olives, pitted, halved
4	ounces	noodles, uncooked (about 2 cups)
2	cups	water
1	teaspoon	oregano leaves
½	teaspoon	salt
¼	teaspoon	pepper
1	cup	cheddar cheese, shredded

Directions:

Cook and stir the meat and onion in a large skillet until the meat is brown. Drain off the excess fat. Stir in the undrained corn and the rest of the ingredients. To cook in a skillet: Heat the mixture to boiling. Then reduce the heat and simmer, uncovered, stirring occasionally, until the noodles are tender, about 20 minutes. Serve hot. To cook in the oven: Pour the mixture into an ungreased 2-quart casserole dish. Cover and bake in a 375F oven for 30 minutes, stirring occasionally. Uncover and bake until the mixture thickens, about 15 minutes. Serve hot.

Macaroni 'n' Cheese with Vegetables

Serves 6

Ingredients:

8	ounces	macaroni (bow-ties, elbow or ribbed)
3	tablespoons	margarine, divided
1	tablespoon	unbleached flour
½	cup	vegetable stock
¾	cup	milk
½	cup	grated cheddar cheese (2 ounces)
½	cup	grated parmesan cheese (2 ounces)
1	tablespoon	chopped fresh parsley
1	teaspoon	basil
¼	teaspoon	paprika
¼	teaspoon	black pepper
2	cups	broccoli florets
1	medium	red pepper, chopped
1	cup	sliced mushrooms (3 ounces)
2		scallions, sliced and curled

Directions:

Bring a large pot of water to a boil. Cook macaroni until done. While macaroni is cooking, in medium saucepan, melt 2 tablespoons of the margarine. Remove from heat, add flour and stir until blended in. Whisk in stock and milk, stirring over medium heat until mixture comes to a boil and thickens. Reduce to low heat. Stir in cheeses and seasonings. Continue stirring until cheese is melted. Remove from heat and set aside. In a large skillet, melt remaining 1 tablespoon margarine. Add remaining ingredients. Cook vegetables, stirring constantly, for about 5 minutes, until tender/crisp. Reduce to low heat. When noodles are done, drain well. Toss with vegetables. Stir in cheese sauce. Garnish with scallion curls.

Pop always had some left-overs in the freezer.

Mom always loved to cook Lasagna.

Lasagna

Courtesy of The National Cattleman's Beef Association
Serves 8

Ingredients:

1	pound	lean ground beef
1	jar (26-32 ounces)	prepared spicy or zesty spaghetti sauce*
1	can (14½-16 ounces)	diced tomatoes, not drained
1	container (15 ounces)	part-skim ricotta cheese
1		egg, well beaten
¼	cup	grated parmesan cheese
1	teaspoon	dried basil leaves, crushed
6		lasagna noodles, uncooked
2	cups (8 ounces)	shredded mozzarella cheese

Directions:

Heat oven to 375F. Cook ground beef in preheated large skillet over medium heat 4 to 6 minutes, or until no longer pink, stirring occasionally to break up ground beef into pea-size pieces. Pour off drippings. Add spaghetti sauce and tomatoes with liquid to skillet, stirring to combine. Reserve.

Meanwhile, combine ricotta cheese, egg, cheese, and basil. Spread 2 cups beef mixture over bottom of 11 x 7½-inch baking dish. Arrange 3 lasagna noodles in single layer, pressing into beef mixture. Spoon ricotta cheese mixture on top of noodles. Sprinkle with 1 cup mozzarella cheese.

Top with additional 2 cups beef mixture. Arrange remaining noodles in single layer, pressing lightly into beef mixture. Top with remaining beef mixture, spreading evenly to cover noodles.

Bake in 375F (moderate) oven 45 minutes, or until noodles are fork tender. Sprinkle remaining 1 cup mozzarella cheese on top; cover with aluminum foil tent. Let stand at least 15 minutes before serving.

* If prepared spicy spaghetti sauce is unavailable, add 1¼ teaspoon ground red pepper to regular prepared spaghetti sauce.

Mom's Asparagus Hot Dish

Serves 4

Ingredients:

2	cups	asparagus, fresh, 2 inch lengths
1	can	cream of mushroom soup
4	ounces	mushrooms, sliced
2	cups	cheddar cheese, grated
1	3 ounce can	french fried onion rings

Directions:

Butter a casserole dish. Put a layer of asparagus on bottom. Then add soup. Next add mushrooms and half the cheese. Add second layer of asparagus and end with a layer of cheese. Bake at 350F for 30 minutes, or until bubbly. Sprinkle onion rings on top and return to oven for 5 minutes more.

Bacon 'n' Egg Hot Dish

Serves 10

Ingredients:

¼	cup	margarine, melted
2	cups	onion/garlic croutons
2	cups	milk
1	tablespoon	prepared mustard
2	cups	unseasoned croutons
2	cups	cheddar cheese, grated
6		eggs
10		slices bacon

Directions:

Cook bacon until it is crispy and crumbly. Coat a 9 x 12 x 2 inch casserole dish with vegetable spray. Place croutons in casserole dish and pour margarine over them. Sprinkle grated cheese over all. Mix milk, eggs, and mustard and pour over cheese. Sprinkle bacon crumbs over all. Bake at 325F for 45 minutes. Allow casserole dish to stand for 15 minutes before serving.

Beef 'n' Cheese Hot Dish

Serves 4

Ingredients:

¼	cup	onion, finely chopped
½	cup	unsalted butter
1	pound	sirloin steak, sliced thinly
2		tomatoes, finely chopped
1		red bell pepper, in ½ inch slices
½		green bell pepper, in ½ inch slices
1	large	egg, hard-boiled, chopped
¼	cup	raisins
¼	cup	black olives, pitted and halved
¼	cup	sweet gherkins, chopped
¼	cup	mushrooms, chopped
2	tablespoons	brandy
2½	teaspoons	flour
½	cup	beef broth
¼	teaspoon	Oriental chili paste
½	teaspoon	chili sauce
½	teaspoon	ketchup
		hot sauce to taste
7	ounces	cheese, sliced ¼ inch thick

sautéed bananas
salt and pepper to taste

Directions:

In a skillet, cook onion in the butter over moderate heat until golden. Add the steak, tomatoes, and bell pepper. Cook, stirring, over moderate-high heat, until vegetables are softened. Add the egg, raisins, olives, gherkins, and mushrooms and cook the mixture, stirring, for 1 minute. Add the heated brandy and ignite. Shake skillet gently until the flames go out. Stir in flour and cook for 2 minutes, stirring. Stir in broth, chili paste, chili sauce, ketchup, hot sauce, and salt and pepper to taste. Simmer the mixture, stirring occasionally, for 5 minutes. Line the sides of a 2 quart shallow casserole dish with some of the cheese slices. Pour the beef mixture into the casserole dish, and cover it with the remaining cheese. Put the casserole dish in a larger pan, add enough water to reach 1 inch up the sides of the casserole dish, and cover the pan with foil. Bake in the middle of a preheated 325F oven for 15 minutes. Serve with sautéed bananas.

Old Fashioned Cabbage Hot Dish

Serves 6

Ingredients:

1	medium	onion, chopped
1	stalk	celery, chopped
3	tablespoons	margarine
¾	pound	lean ground beef
½	teaspoon	salt
1		medium cabbage, shredded
2		apples, sliced thin

Directions:

Preheat your oven to 350F. In skillet, sauté onion and celery in margarine for 2 minutes. Add beef and salt and stir another 2 minutes. Spread half the cabbage in 2 quart baking dish and cover with half the apples and all the meat mixture. Add remaining cabbage and apple slices. Cover and bake 1 hour. Nice with mashed potatoes or noodles.

Grandma's Favorite Cauliflower Hot Dish

Serves 6

Ingredients:

1	medium	cauliflower, broken into florets
4		potatoes, large, peeled and diced
1	tablespoons	butter or margarine
3		eggs
¾	cup	hard Swiss cheese
1	tablespoon	salt, to taste
1	teaspoon	pepper to taste
1	teaspoon	cayenne pepper

Directions:

Cook the cauliflower in boiling salted water for 15 minutes or until tender. Meanwhile, cook the potatoes in boiling water for 15 minutes or longer, until tender. Drain the potatoes and cauliflower, and place in mixing bowl. Add the butter, salt, and pepper. Mash together to make a puree. It is better to use a potato masher, as a food processor can make it too mushy. Beat the eggs into the puree, one at a time. Then stir in the cheese, reserving 2 tablespoons of the cheese. Spoon into a greased dish, and bake for 50 to 60 minutes at 375F with foil over it.

Before serving, sprinkle the remaining cheese on top and put under the broiler. This can be prepared in the morning and put in the refrigerator.

Home-Made Beef Pie

Serves 6

Ingredients:

1	pound	ground beef
1	small	package of cream cheese
1	can	mushroom soup
1	cup	canned corn with pimento
1	package	refrigerated biscuits

Directions:

Brown ground beef in skillet. Drain. Mix all but biscuits. Pour in 2 quart casserole dish. Top with biscuits. Bake at 350F for about 20 minutes.

Ham 'n' Cheese Hot Dish

Serves 8

Ingredients:

1	10 ounce pack	green beans, french cut
4	tablespoons	butter
¼	cup	onion, minced
4	tablespoons	all-purpose flour
½	teaspoon	salt
1½	cups	milk
2	cups	ham, cooked, chopped
2		eggs, hard-cooked, chopped
1	cup	cheddar cheese, shredded
2	tablespoons	pimento, chopped
1	tablespoon	parsley, chopped
½	cup	croutons, herb-flavored, crushed

Directions:

Cook the beans according to package directions. Drain and reserve ½ cup liquid. Melt the butter in a 2-quart saucepan. Sauté onion. Stir in flour and salt until well blended.

Remove from heat. Stir in milk and reserved½ cup liquid. Heat to a boil, stirring constantly. Boil and stir 1 minute.

Remove from heat. Stir in ham, eggs, cheese, pimento, and parsley. Place beans in baking dish. Cover with ham sauce and sprinkle croutons over top.

Bake in preheated 350F oven for 20 to 25 minutes.

Chicken Hot Dish with Mushrooms

Serves 6

Ingredients:

4	pounds	chicken
16	ounces	bottled Italian dressing
6	cups	white wine
1	pound	fresh mushrooms
2	cloves	garlic
4	cans	chicken gravy (10½ ounces)

Directions:

Remove skin and bones from chicken and cut into bite sized pieces. Trim mushrooms and cut in half. In large casserole dish, combine chicken, mushrooms, whole garlic cloves, wine, and dressing. Cover and marinate in refrigerator overnight. Remove chicken and mushrooms and measure 2 cups of marinade. Pour remaining marinade into another container. Return chicken and mushrooms to casserole dish. Mix 2 cups marinade with cans of gravy and pour over chicken. Bake at 250F for 1½ hours.

This hot dish may be served hot over rice, potatoes, or biscuits. Remaining marinade can be frozen for later use as marinade or for a barbeque.

Chicken Hot Dish with Rice

Serves 6

Ingredients:

¼	cup	margarine
¼	cup	all-purpose flour
¾	teaspoon	salt
¼	teaspoon	pepper
1½	cups	milk
1	cup	chicken broth
2	cups	cut-up cooked chicken or turkey
1½	cups	cooked white or wild rice
¼	cup	chopped green bell pepper
¼	cup	slivered almonds
2	tablespoons	chopped pimento
1	4 ounces can	mushroom stems and pieces, drained
	or	
1	cup	chopped mushrooms

parsley for garnish if desired

Directions:
Heat oven to 350F. Heat margarine in 2-quart saucepan until melted. Stir in flour, salt, and pepper. Cook over medium heat, stirring constantly, until bubbly. Remove from heat. Stir in milk and broth. Heat to boiling, stirring constantly. Boil and stir 1 minute. Stir in remaining ingredients. Pour into ungreased 2-quart casserole dish

or rectangular baking dish, 10 x 6 x 1½ inches. Bake uncovered 40 to 45 minutes, or until bubbly. Garnish with parsley if desired.

Grandma's Chicken Hot Dish

Serves 5

Ingredients:

½	cup	margarine
4		chicken breasts, cooked and boned
1	package	stuffing mix (6 ounce)
1	can	cream of mushroom soup
1	can	cream of chicken soup
2	cups	chicken broth

Directions:
Melt margarine and combine with stuffing mix and mushroom soup that has been diluted with 1 cup of the chicken broth. Place ½ of the mixture in 9 x 13 inch baking dish. Layer chicken. Pour mushroom soup that has been diluted with other cup of chicken broth over top. Bake at 350F for about 1 hour.

Home-Made Chicken Pot Pie

Serves 4 to 6

Ingredients:

10	ounces	peas and carrots
½	cup	chopped onions
½	cup	chopped mushrooms
¼	cup	margarine or butter
¼	cup	all-purpose flour
½	teaspoon	salt
½	teaspoon	dried sage or thyme
¼	teaspoon	pepper
2	cups	chicken broth
¾	cups	milk
3	cups	cooked chicken (or turkey)
¼	cup	snipped parsley

Pastry shells, double crust, prebaked

Directions:
Cook peas and carrots and drain. Set aside. Cook mushrooms and onions in margarine or butter until tender. Stir in flour, salt, sage or thyme, and pepper. Add chicken broth and milk. Cook and stir until thick. Stir in peas and carrots, chicken (or turkey), and parsley. Heat until bubbly. Pour into shell(s) that are in a pie or casserole dish. Cook in oven at 450F for 12 to 15 minutes or until pastry is golden brown. Prebaked home-made (see page 96) or store bought pie shells are needed. If desired use 1 large or several individual size pie crusts.

Mom often had a couple of casseroles in the oven.

We always looked forward to Chicken and Spaghetti.

Chicken and Spaghetti

Courtesy of The National Broiler Council
  Serves 6

Ingredients:

8		broiler-fryer chicken parts
3	tablespoons	olive oil
1		clove garlic, split
½	cup	chopped celery
½	cup	chopped onion
¼	cup	chopped green pepper
1	teaspoon	salt
½	teaspoon	pepper
1	can (15 ounces)	tomato sauce
1	can (15 ounces)	Italian plum tomatoes, drained, liquid reserved
1	teaspoon	parsley
½	teaspoon	basil
½	teaspoon	oregano
1		chicken bouillon cube
½	cup	hot water
1		bay leaf
12	ounces	vermicelli
½	cup	shredded mozzarella cheese

Directions:

In dutch oven, place olive oil and garlic; heat to medium high temperature. Add chicken and cook, turning, about 10 minutes or until brown on all sides. Add celery, onion, and green pepper; stir until onion is clear, about 5 minutes. Sprinkle chicken with salt and pepper. In blender container, pour tomato sauce and drained liquid from plum tomatoes. Add parsley, basil, and oregano; blend for 1 minute and pour over chicken. In small bowl, place hot water and bouillon cube; let stand until bouillon cube is dissolved. Add bouillon and bay leaf to chicken. Cut plum tomatoes in half and add to chicken. Cook at medium low temperature, uncovered, about 30 minutes until liquid is slightly thickened and fork can be inserted in chicken with ease. Prepare vermicelli according to package instructions. In large serving bowl, arrange cooked noodles; place chicken over noodles and pour sauce over all. Sprinkle with cheese.

Grandma's Special Chicken 'n' Stuffing Hot Dish

Serves 6

Ingredients:

¼	cup	oil
½	cup	flour
½	teaspoon	paprika
¼	teaspoon	pepper
3½	pounds	broiler-fryer chicken, cut up
1	can	condensed cream of chicken or cream of mushroom soup
6	cups	soft bread cubes (about 10 slices)
¼	cup	butter, melted
1	cup	milk
¾	teaspoon	salt
½	teaspoon	rubbed sage
½	teaspoon	dried thyme leaves
¼	teaspoon	pepper
1		large stalk celery, chopped (about ¾ cup)
1		medium onion, chopped (about ½ cup)

Directions:

Heat oil over medium heat in 10 inch skillet. Mix flour, paprika, and ¼ teaspoon of pepper. Coat chicken with flour mixture. Cook chicken in oil over medium heat for 15 to 20 minutes or until brown. Heat oven to 350F. Place chicken in ungreased 2½ quart casserole dish or square baking dish, 9 x 9 x 2 inches. Pour soup over chicken. Toss remaining ingredients. Mound mixture on chicken. Cover and bake 1 hour to 1 hour and 15 minutes, or until chicken is done.

Easy Corned Beef Hot Dish

Serves 6 to 8

Ingredients:

8	ounces	uncooked elbow macaroni
2	cans	chicken and mushroom soup
2½	cups	milk
12	ounces	canned corned beef
1½	cups	grated cheddar cheese
2	small	sautéed onions, chopped
1	cup	buttered bread crumbs

Directions:

Mix all ingredients and let stand overnight in refrigerator, or for at least 12 hours. Cover with buttered crumbs and pour into a large casserole dish. Bake 1½ hours at 350F.

Mom's Hamburger Hot Dish

Serves 6

Ingredients:

1	pound	lean hamburger
¼	teaspoon	pepper
1	tablespoon	butter
¼	cup	onion, minced
¼	teaspoon	garlic
16	ounces	tomato sauce (2 cans)
1	teaspoon	salt
1	cup	sour cream
1	cup	cottage cheese, creamed
1¼	cups	carrots, sliced
8	ounces	medium sized noodles, cooked and drained
1	cup	cheddar, medium, shredded

Directions:

Brown the hamburger in the butter and add the onions and garlic. Stir in the tomato sauce, salt, and pepper. Combine the sour cream, cheese, and carrots. Add the combination to the noodles and mix. Alternate layers of the meat mixture and the noodle mixture in a 3-quart casserole dish, beginning and ending with the noodle mixture. Top with the cheddar cheese. Bake at 350F for at least 45 minutes and serve hot.

Easy Noodle Casserole

Serves 6

Ingredients:

¾	cup	skim milk
1½	tablespoons	cornstarch
2	tablespoons	minced fresh parsley
1	dash	Worcestershire sauce
2	cups	tender cooked medium egg noodles, drained
16	ounces	low fat cottage cheese
½	cup	plain low fat yogurt
1	4 ounce can	drained mushroom pieces
1		minced onion
		salt and pepper to taste
1	pinch	cayenne pepper
1	pinch	dry mustard
5	tablespoons	grated sharp American cheese (optional)
2	tablespoons	seasoned bread crumbs

Directions:

Blend milk and cornstarch in a saucepan. Cook mixture over low heat, stirring constantly, until it simmers and thickens. Stir in parsley, Worcestershire sauce, cayenne, and mustard. In non stick baking dish, combine milk mixture with noodles, cottage cheese, yogurt, mushrooms, onion, salt and pepper. Sprinkle top with grated cheese and bread crumbs. Bake, uncovered, in preheated 350F oven for 30 minutes.

Pop's Favorite Beef 'n' Noodle Hot Dish

Serves 5

Ingredients:

4	ounces	dried beef, snipped
2	cups	water
1		small onion, chopped
2	cups	uncooked noodles
1	can	cream of mushroom soup 10¾ ounce size can, condensed
½	cup	milk
1	teaspoon	dried parsley flakes
4	ounces	(1 cup) shredded cheddar cheese

Directions:
Cover and microwave dried beef and 1 cup water in 2 quart casserole dish on high (100%) to boiling, 2 to 3 minutes. Drain. Stir in onion, noodles, soup, milk, second cup of water and parsley flakes. Cover and microwave 10 minutes. Stir. Cover and microwave until noodles are tender, 5 to 6 minutes. Stir in cheese. Cover and microwave until melted, 2 to 3 minutes. Let stand 5 minutes before serving.

Home-Style Barbequed Chicken Hot Dish

Serves 4

Ingredients:

1	can	pork and beans (16 ounces)
4		chicken pieces
¼	cup	ketchup
2	tablespoons	peach preserves
2	teaspoons	onion, instant, minced
¼	teaspoon	soy sauce
¼	cup	brown sugar

Directions:
Place beans in a 2-quart casserole dish. Top with the chicken pieces. Mix together remaining ingredients. Pour over chicken and beans. Cover and bake in preheated 325F oven for 1¾ hours.

Onion 'n' Green Bean Casserole

Serves 6

Ingredients:

3	tablespoons	butter
3	tablespoons	flour
1	tablespoon	mustard, prepared yellow
½	teaspoon	salt
¼	teaspoon	hot sauce
1	16 ounce can	green beans, undrained milk
1	16 ounce can	onions, small whole, drained
1	cup	crushed potato chips

Directions:
Melt butter. Add flour, stirring until smooth. Add mustard, salt, hot sauce, and bean liquid, plus milk, to make 1½ cups. Cook until thick. Add beans and drained onions. Place in a greased 1 quart casserole dish. Border with buttered and lightly crushed potato chips. Bake in preheated 375F oven for 30 minutes, or until potato chips brown.

Basic Green Bean Casserole

Serves 4

Ingredients:

1	can	green beans, french style
1	can	cream of mushroom soup
1	can	french fried onion rings

Directions:
In casserole dish mix beans and soup. Top with onion rings. Heat in moderate oven for 20 minutes.

Noodles with Ham

Serves 2

Ingredients:

¼	cup	skim milk
1		egg, separated
1	tablespoon	margarine, melted, divided
¼	teaspoon	pepper
5	ounces	boiled ham, cut into ½-inch cubes
1	cup	cooked noodles (medium width)
1	dash	salt

Directions:

Preheat your oven to 375F. In small mixing bowl combine milk, egg yolk, 2½ teaspoons margarine, and pepper, mixing thoroughly. Add ham and noodles and stir well to thoroughly combine. In separate bowl beat egg white with salt until stiff but not dry. Gently fold into noodle mixture. Grease 2 quart casserole dish with remaining margarine and spoon noodle mixture into casserole dish. Bake until browned on top, 45 to 50 minutes.

Hamburger Hot Dish

Serves 10

Ingredients:

2	cups	noodles
1	can	tomato soup
1	can	mushroom soup
1	cup	celery
1	cup	water
1	pound	hamburger
1		onion
1	cup	grated cheese

Directions:

Boil noodles in water until done according to package. Cook celery in 1 cup water. Brown hamburger and onions together. Pour noodles, celery and liquid in 2 to 3 quart casserole dish. Add mushroom soup, tomato soup and grated cheese. Save enough cheese to sprinkle on top. Bake at 350F for 1 hour. Serve with green salad and hot biscuits.

Lima Beans 'n' Chops

Serves 4

Ingredients:

4		lamb or pork chops
1	dash	salt
1	dash	pepper
3	cups	lima beans, drained (save liquid)
1	teaspoon	oil
½	cup	hot water
½	cup	tomato ketchup
1		onion, chopped

Directions:

Season chops to taste with the salt and pepper. Brown in oil with onion. Place lima beans and chops in layers in an ovenproof casserole dish. Add hot water to pan drippings with ketchup and bring to a boil. Pour over layered casserole. Add the bean liquid as needed while baking in the oven. Bake at 350F for 1½ hours.

Sometimes mom cooked a casserole as a side dish.

Nobody ever skipped dinner when we were having Tomato and Potato Casserole.

Tomato and Potato Casserole

Courtesy of The Florida Tomatoes
  Serves 4-6

Layers of potatoes simmer gently between layers of tomatoes in this aromatic main dish. The semolina helps to thicken the juice thrown off by the tomatoes, leaving a broth with lots of body and flavor.

Ingredients:

½	cup	freshly grated parmesan cheese
2	tablespoons	semolina
2	tablespoons	chopped fresh oregano
or		
2	teaspoons	dried oregano
4		large Florida tomatoes, cored and sliced ¼ inch thick
6 to 8		medium-size all-purpose potatoes, very thinly sliced
1	small	onion, minced

salt and freshly ground pepper to taste

Directions:

Preheat the oven to 400F and butter a deep, 10 inch, round casserole dish or gratin dish. In a small bowl, mix the parmesan cheese, semolina, and oregano and set aside.

To assemble, put a layer of tomatoes in the bottom of the casserole dish, salt and pepper lightly, then cover with about 2 tablespoons of the parmesan mixture. Put a layer of slightly overlapping potatoes on top of the tomatoes. Salt and pepper lightly and sprinkle with minced onion. Continue this layering, ending with the tomatoes and cheese mixture.

Cover the casserole dish with foil and bake for about 1¼ to 1½ hours, until the potatoes are tender. Uncover, then let the dish sit for 5 minutes before serving.

Pork Chop Hot Dish

Serves 4

Ingredients:

1		onion soup mix package
¾	cup	water
2	tablespoons	brown sugar
½	teaspoon	cinnamon
¼	teaspoon	nutmeg
4	cups	thinly sliced potatoes
2		medium onions
4		apples cut in ½ inch rings
4		thick pork chops

Directions:

Combine soup mix, water, brown sugar, and spices. Set aside. Put the potatoes, onions, apples, and pork chops in a shallow baking dish. Pour brown sugar mixture over potato mixture. Bake 1½ hours at 375F.

Spaghetti Hot Dish

Serves 8

Ingredients:

1½	cups	ground chuck
1	large	onion, chopped
1	large	green pepper, chopped
½	pound	fresh mushrooms, sliced
2	cloves	garlic, minced
1	can	35 ounces peeled tomatoes, coarsely chopped (save juice)
1	12 ounce can	tomato sauce
1	teaspoon	basil
1	teaspoon	oregano
1		bay leaf
¾	teaspoon	salt
¼	teaspoon	pepper
1	pound	spaghetti or fettuccine
2	cups	shredded cheddar cheese
1	cup	lightly crushed potato chips

Directions:

In a 5-6 quart dutch oven, cook the ground chuck, onion, peppers, mushrooms, and garlic over medium-high heat, stirring often to break up lumps of meat, until beef loses its pink color (about 8 minutes). Add tomatoes with their juice, tomato sauce, basil, oregano, bay leaf, salt and pepper. Bring to a boil. Reduce heat to medium-low and simmer, stirring often, until slightly thickened, about 20 minutes.

Meanwhile, in a large pot of lightly salted water, cook spaghetti until just tender, about 9 minutes. Drain well.

Preheat your oven to 350F. Add spaghetti, and 1 cup of cheese, to the sauce. Stir gently to mix. Transfer to a lightly oiled, very large baking dish. Sprinkle with lightly crushed potato chips and remaining cheese on top. Bake until top is lightly browned and casserole dish is bubbling, about 30 minutes. Let stand 5 minutes before serving.
Note: One can of sliced black olives may be added to the sauce with the spaghetti.

Mom's Corn Casserole

Serves 6 to 8

Ingredients:

1	pound	bacon, diced
2	cups	lightly crushed potato chips
¼	cup	minced onion
2	cans	cream style corn (16½ ounce each)

Directions:

In a skillet, fry the bacon until lightly browned. Remove and set aside. Pour ¼ to ½ cup of the bacon drippings over lightly crushed potato chips. Set aside. Discard all but 2 tablespoons of remaining drippings. Sauté onion until tender. Stir in corn and bacon. Spoon into a 1 quart baking dish. Sprinkle with potato chips. Bake at 350F for 20-25 minutes, or until bubbly and heated through.

Chili-Cheese Hot Dish

Serves 6

Ingredients:

8	ounces	diced green chilies (2 cans)
1	pound	Monterey Jack cheese, grated
1	pound	cheddar cheese, grated
4		eggs, separated
¾	cup	canned evaporated milk
1	tablespoon	flour
½	teaspoon	salt
¼	teaspoon	pepper
2	medium	tomatoes, sliced
1	can	green chilies

Directions:

Preheat your oven to 325F. In large bowl, combine green chilies and cheeses. Place in a well-buttered, shallow, 12 x 9 inch 2 quart casserole dish. Beat egg whites just until stiff peaks form. Combine yolks, milk, flour, salt, and pepper, mixing until well blended. Using rubber spatula, gently fold beaten whites into yolk mixture. Pour egg mixture over cheese mixture in casserole dish, using a fork to push it through the cheese. Bake 30 minutes. Remove from oven and arrange sliced tomatoes overlapping around outer edges. Bake 30 minutes longer, or until a knife inserted in center comes out clean. Garnish with chopped green chilies, if desired. Serve with chips, salsa, and refried beans.

Mom's Potato Hot Dish

Serves 12

Ingredients:

2	pounds	frozen hash brown potatoes
½	cup	margarine, melted
½	cup	chopped green onions
1	pint	sour cream
1	can	creamy onion soup
1	teaspoon	salt
2	cups	shredded cheddar cheese
¼	teaspoon	pepper
¼	cup	margarine
2	cups	cornflakes, crushed

Directions:

Thaw potatoes and combine with ½ cup margarine, salt, pepper, onions, soup, sour cream, and cheese. Place in a greased 9 x 13 inch casserole dish. Combine cornflakes and remaining ¼ cup margarine. Spread over potato mixture. Bake at 350F for 45 to 60 minutes.

Grandma's Potato and Cabbage Hot Dish

Serves 4

Ingredients:

1½	pounds	potatoes, unpeeled (3 large)
		water, boiling
½	pound	bacon, cut into 3 inch strips
1	cup	onion, sliced
2	tablespoons	flour
½	teaspoon	thyme, dried
½	teaspoon	salt
1½	cups	beer (12 ounces)
½	cup	milk
6	cups	cabbage, fine shredded (1½ pounds)
1	cup	Swiss cheese, shredded

Directions:

Steam potatoes in 1 inch boiling water 30 to 40 minutes, or until tender.
Slice potatoes, unpeeled, into ½ slices. Set aside.
Cook bacon in a large skillet until crisp. Set aside.
Pour off all but 2 tablespoons bacon fat, sauté onion in same skillet until golden. Stir in flour, thyme and salt.

Gradually add beer and milk. Stir over low heat, until mixture boils and thickens.
In 3-quart casserole dish, layer half the cabbage, potatoes, bacon, cheese, and sauce. Repeat with remaining ingredients.
Cover and bake in preheated 375F oven for 30 minutes. Uncover and bake 15 minutes longer, or until cabbage is tender.

Easy Baked Macaroni

Serves 4

Ingredients:

1	pound	macaroni
1	tablespoon	vegetable oil
1		onion, chopped
1	can	tomatoes (28 ounces) crushed
1	teaspoon	oregano, dried
1	dash	salt and pepper
2	cups	cheese, grated, any type

Directions:

Preheat oven to 325F. Cook macaroni on stove and drain. Meanwhile, heat oil in saucepan. Add onion and garlic. Sauté until soft (about 5 minutes). Add tomatoes, oregano, salt, and pepper. Cook until heated through, about 5 minutes. Combine cooked macaroni, sauce, and 1 cup grated cheese in oven proof dish. Sprinkle remaining cheese on top. Bake 15-20 minutes at 350F. Omit onions and garlic for even quicker rendition.

Sweet Potato Hot Dish

Serves 8

Ingredients:

6		sweet potatoes
½	cup	butter
1	5.3-ounce can	evaporated milk
1		orange (grated zest only)
¼	cup	sherry
½	cup	brown sugar
2		egg whites
½	cup	pecans, chopped fine
3	tablespoons	melted butter

Directions:

Cook potatoes in boiling water until tender. Peel while still hot. Place in large mixing bowl and mash well.
Beat with electric mixer at medium speed and gradually add butter, milk, orange zest, sherry, and brown sugar.
Beat egg whites until stiff and gently fold into potato mixture. Pour into buttered casserole dish.
Sprinkle top with chopped pecans that have been mixed with melted butter. Bake at 350F for 30 minutes.

Grandma's Tuna Casserole

Serves 4

Ingredients:

1	can	cream of mushroom soup
½	cup	milk
6	½ ounces	tuna, drained and flaked
2		eggs, hard boiled, sliced
1	cup	peas, cooked
1	cup	lightly crushed potato chips

Directions:

Preheat your oven to 350F. Slightly crumble the potato chips. Blend soup and milk in 1-quart casserole dish. Stir in tuna, eggs, and peas. Bake 20 minutes. Top with chips. Bake 10 minutes longer. You may use tuna packed in oil or water.

Mom's Zucchini Hot Dish

Serves 4

Ingredients:

6	cups	sliced zucchini
½	cup	chopped onion
1	can	cream of chicken soup
1	cup	sour cream
4	ounces	shredded sharp cheddar cheese
8	ounce	package of herb seasoned stuffing
½	cup	melted butter

Directions:

Cook zucchini in water until just tender, crisp. Do not overcook. Drain and combine other ingredients. Combine stuffing mix with melted butter. Put half in

If mom 'n' pop were going out, she'd whip up something quick.

bottom of buttered casserole dish. Put zucchini mixture over this. Top with remaining stuffing mix. Bake at 350F for 1 hour.

Our Favorite Baked Beans

Serves 4

Ingredients:

2	cups	pork and beans (16 ounce cans)
¼	cup	bottled barbeque sauce
¼	cup	brown sugar
¼	cup	golden raisins
½	cup	tart apples
½	cup	chopped onion
8		bacon strips

Directions:

Drain pork and beans and place in ovenproof bowl. Chop onion and apples and add to beans. Also add barbeque sauce, brown sugar, and raisins. Mix together and lay bacon strips on top. Place in covered grill and bake at 350F for 1 to 1½ hours.

Basic Baked Beans 'n' Ground Beef

Serves 24

Ingredients:

1	pound	ground beef
½	pound	smoked bacon
¾	cup	green pepper, chopped
1	cup	onions, chopped
8	ounces	tomato sauce
¼	cup	mustard
4	tablespoons	liquid hickory smoke
1	cup	water
4	tablespoons	vinegar
2	teaspoons	garlic, minced
1	teaspoon	thyme
¾	cup	brown sugar
32	ounces	pork n' beans

salt and pepper to taste

Directions:

In a large frying pan, cook ground beef in its own fat. Add green pepper and onion. Sauté until beef is brown and vegetables are limp. Set aside 4 strips of bacon. Cut the remaining bacon into 2-inch strips and add to ground beef mixture. Stir in the tomato sauce, water, vinegar, garlic, mustard, thyme, brown sugar, liquid hickory smoke, and salt and pepper to taste. Simmer together 5 minutes. Place pork n' beans in a greased 1½ quart baking dish. Spoon meat mixture over top. Place remaining strips of bacon over top of ground beef. Bake at 375F for 45 minutes.

Green Bean Casserole

Serves 6

Ingredients:

1	cup	cream of mushroom soup
½	cup	milk
1	teaspoon	soy sauce
1	dash	pepper
4	cups	cooked green beans
1	can	french fried onions

Directions:
In 1½ quart casserole dish, combine soup, milk, soy sauce, and pepper. Stir in beans and ½ can onions.
Bake at 350F for 25 minutes, or until hot. Stir. Top with remaining onions.

Cheese and Spinach Strudel is great with Tomato Relish.

Cheese and Spinach Strudel with Warm Tomato Relish

Courtesy of The Florida Tomatoes
Serves 6

Ingredients:

1	10 ounce package	frozen chopped spinach
½	pound	ricotta cheese
1	cup	grated mozzarella cheese
½	cup	freshly grated parmesan cheese
2	pinches	of ground nutmeg
6		sheets phyllo dough, each measuring 14 x 18 inches
3	tablespoons	unsalted butter

fine dry bread crumbs
salt and freshly ground pepper to taste

Warm tomato relish:

2	tablespoons	olive oil
1		small onion, minced
1		celery rib, minced
4	large	Florida tomatoes, cored, seeded, and coarsely chopped
½	cup	grated carrot
1	teaspoon	fresh thyme
or		
½	teaspoon	dried thyme
1	teaspoon	fresh lemon juice
2	teaspoons	chopped fresh parsley

salt and freshly ground pepper to taste

Directions:
Cook the spinach according to the package directions and cool on a plate. Squeeze out the excess moisture by hand and mix with the cheeses in a bowl. Stir in the nutmeg and salt and pepper to taste. Preheat the oven to 375F.
To assemble, lay a sheet of phyllo on your work surface with a short edge facing you. Brush it lightly with butter and sprinkle with crumbs. Repeat this layering until all the sheets of phyllo are used.
About 3 inches in from the short edge facing you, arrange the filling in a mounded row about 3 inches wide, leaving 3 inches uncovered along each long edge so you can fold the sides over. Fold the sides of the phyllo over the filling, then fold the short end of exposed phyllo over the filling. Continue to roll the phyllo into a log. Poke 2 small steam vents in the top with a knife. Place the strudel on a baking sheet and bake for 30 to 40 minutes, until golden brown.
While the strudel bakes, make the relish. Heat the oil in a medium-size saucepan. Stir in the onion and celery and sauté over medium heat for 3 minutes. Stir in the tomatoes, carrot, thyme, and salt and pepper to taste. Simmer the relish gently until most of the liquid has cooked off. Remove from the heat.
Right before serving, rewarm the relish. Remove from the heat and stir in the lemon juice and parsley. Slice the strudel and serve hot with some of the relish spooned around each slice.

Mom'n'Pop's
Chicken and Poultry Recipes

Mom's Baked Chicken

Serves 8

Ingredients:

2		fryer chickens (2½ pounds)
½	cup	olive oil
1	large	onion, minced
1	clove	garlic, minced
1	teaspoon	salt
¾	teaspoon	pepper
1		medium tomato, chopped
	or	
½	cup	drained canned tomatoes
½	cup	white wine, dry

Directions:
Cut the chickens in quarters. In dutch oven or heavy kettle, brown chickens in olive oil until golden brown. Add onion, garlic, salt, and pepper. Cover and simmer for 30 minutes. Add tomato (may substitute ½ cup drained canned tomatoes) and wine and simmer for 30 minutes longer, or until chicken is tender.

Mom's Crispy Fried Chicken

Serves 4

Ingredients:

¾	pound	boneless chicken pieces
2	cups	oil
½	cup	all-purpose flour

Marinade:

1	teaspoon	chili bean sauce, or chili powder
2	teaspoons	rice wine or dry sherry
1	teaspoon	light soy sauce
1	teaspoon	dark soy sauce
2	teaspoons	finely chopped ginger
1	tablespoon	finely chopped scallions
1	teaspoon	granulated sugar

Directions:
Cut chicken into strips 2 inches by ½ inch and place in a large bowl. Blend the marinade ingredients together and pour the mixture over the chicken. Mix well to ensure an even distribution. Allow the chicken to marinate for 30 to 40 minutes at room temperature. Heat the oil in a deep-fat fryer or large wok until it is quite hot. Lightly sprinkle the chicken strips with the flour and deep-fry for 8 minutes. Remove and drain on paper towels. Serve at once.

Home-Style Drumsticks

Serves 4

Ingredients:

8		chicken drumsticks, skinned (about 2½ pounds)
1½	cups	lightly crushed potato chips
¼	cup	grated parmesan cheese
2	tablespoons	minced fresh parsley
¼	teaspoon	garlic powder
¼	teaspoon	pepper
¼	cup	skim milk

Directions:
Rinse chicken thoroughly with cold water and pat dry. Combine lightly crushed potato chips and other ingredients (except milk), stirring well. Dip drumsticks in skim milk. Dredge in potato chip mixture, coating well. Place drumsticks in a 10 x 6 x 2 inch greased baking dish. Bake at 350F for 1 hour, or until tender.

Oven-Fried Chicken

Serves 6

Ingredients:

¼	cup	margarine or butter
½	cup	all-purpose flour

1	teaspoon	paprika
1/2	teaspoon	salt
1/4	teaspoon	pepper
3	pounds	fryer chicken, cut up

Directions:

Heat oven to 425F. Melt margarine in rectangular pan, 13 x 9 x 2 inches, in oven. Mix flour, paprika, salt, and pepper. Coat chicken with flour mixture. Place chicken, skin side down, in pan. Bake uncovered 30 minutes. Turn chicken and bake about 30 minutes longer.

Grandma's Famous Cornflake Chicken

Serves 4

Ingredients:

3	pounds	fryer chicken, cut up
2		eggs, large, slightly beaten
4	tablespoons	milk
2½	cups	cornflakes, crushed
2	teaspoons	salt
1/2	teaspoon	pepper
5	tablespoons	butter, melted

Directions:

Preheat your oven to 350F. Crush but do not pulverize the cornflakes. Wash chicken and pat dry. Mix together eggs and milk. Separately mix cornflake crumbs, salt, and pepper. Dip chicken into milk and egg mixture and then into the crumb mixture, coating each piece evenly. Set in well-greased baking pan. Coat with melted butter. Bake, uncovered, for 1 hour.

Oven-Barbequed Chicken

Serves 6

Ingredients:

3-3½	pounds	broiler-fryer chicken, cut up
3/4	cup	chili sauce
2	tablespoons	honey
2	tablespoons	soy sauce
1	teaspoon	dry mustard
1/2	teaspoon	prepared horseradish
1/2	teaspoon	red pepper sauce

Directions:

Heat oven to 375F. Place chicken, skin side up, in ungreased rectangular pan, 13 x 9 x 2 inches. Mix remaining ingredients. Pour over chicken. Cover and bake 30 minutes. Spoon sauce over chicken. Bake uncovered 30 minutes longer, or until drippings are clear.

Oven-Barbequed Turkey Drumsticks

Serves 6

Ingredients:

1/4	cup	flour
1	teaspoon	salt
1/2	teaspoon	chili powder
1/4	teaspoon	pepper
6		turkey legs, small
1/4	cup	corn oil
1/2	cup	barbeque sauce
1/2	cup	water
1		chicken bouillon cube, crushed

Directions:

Mix flour with salt, chili powder, and pepper. Dredge turkey legs with flour mixture. Heat oil in a large skillet. Brown turkey, turning to brown all sides. Remove turkey to a 13 x 9 x 2 inch pan. Combine barbeque sauce, water, and bouillon cube. Spoon over turkey. Cover pan with foil. Bake in preheated 325F oven for 1 hour. Uncover and bake 1 hour, until turkey is tender, basting frequently.

Note: Oven barbequed drumsticks are delicious with pan-baked potato halves, fresh zucchini and a hot peach or pear half.

Crisp Baked Chicken with Creamy Onion Dressing

Courtesy of The National Broiler Council
Serves 4

Ingredients:

8		broiler-fryer chicken parts
½	cup	fresh lemon juice
½	cup	water
2	teaspoons	sugar
2	teaspoons	olive oil
1¼	teaspoons	salt, divided
¼	teaspoon	garlic powder
¼	teaspoon	coarsely-ground pepper
½	cup	French onion/sour cream dip
½	cup	mayonnaise
1	tablespoon	brown, coarse grain mustard

Directions:

In small saucepan mix together lemon juice, water, sugar, olive oil, ¼ teaspoon of the salt, garlic powder and pepper. Place over high temperature and bring to boil; cook, stirring, about 1 minute and remove from heat. Dip chicken, one piece at a time, in lemon mixture, turning to coat. Arrange chicken in single layer in greased 9 x 13 inch baking pan. Place in 375F oven and bake, turning and basting with lemon mixture every 15 minutes, for about 1 hour, or until fork can be inserted in chicken with ease. In small bowl, mix together ½ cup French onion sour cream dip, ½ cup

mayonnaise and 1 tablespoon brown coarse-grain mustard. Cover and refrigerate.

Game-Time Broiled Chili Chicken

Courtesy of The National Broiler Council
Serves 6

Ingredients:

12		broiler-fryer chicken drumsticks, skinned
½	cup	butter-flavored margarine, melted
1	tablespoon	chili powder
1	tablespoon	chopped cilantro, stems included
3	tablespoons	fresh lemon juice
1	clove	garlic
1	teaspoon	salt

Directions:

In blender, place melted margarine, chili powder, cilantro, lemon juice, and garlic; blend 30 seconds and pour mixture into shallow bowl. Place drumsticks, one at a time, in blended mixture and turn to coat. Arrange drumsticks on broiler pan and sprinkle with ½ teaspoon of the salt. Set temperature on broil with rack about 7 inches from heat. Broil chicken, turning and basting, about 40 minutes, or until fork can be inserted with ease. After first turning, sprinkle chicken with remaining ½ teaspoon of the salt.

Mom always cooked up some Game-Time Broiled Chili Chicken to take to the ballpark.

Crisp Baked Chicken is perfect with Creamy Onion Dressing.

Home-Style Chicken in Cream Gravy

Serves 4

Ingredients:

1		egg, slightly beaten
1	cup	all-purpose flour
2	teaspoons	garlic salt
1	teaspoon	paprika
1	teaspoon	black pepper
1/4	teaspoon	poultry seasoning
3	pounds	fryer chicken, cut up
3	cups	shortening or oil
1	cup	chicken stock
1	cup	milk

Directions:
Combine milk and egg in medium bowl. Combine flour, garlic salt, paprika, pepper, and poultry seasoning in paper or plastic bag. Add a few pieces of chicken at a time, and shake to coat. Dip chicken in milk-egg mixture, then shake a second time in flour mixture. Reserve remainder of the flour. Heat 1/2 to 1 inch of shortening or oil to 365F in electric skillet, or on medium-high burner in a large, heavy skillet. Brown chicken on all sides. Reduce heat to medium-low, or 275F. Continue cooking until chicken is tender, about 30 to 40 minutes. Turn chicken several times during cooking, and drain on paper towels in a single layer. To make the gravy, pour all but 2 tablespoons of the fat from the skillet. Stir in 2 tablespoons of the reserved seasoned flour, and stir constantly over low heat for 2 minutes. Whisk in the chicken stock, stirring to scrape up the brown bits on the bottom of the pan. Then stir in the milk and bring to a boil over high heat, stirring constantly. Reduce the heat to low, and simmer for 5 minutes. Serve immediately, passing the gravy separately.

Spicy Chicken 'n' Noodles

Serves 4

Ingredients:

2		chicken breasts
1/2	teaspoon	oregano
1/2	teaspoon	basil
1/4	teaspoon	pepper
1		onion, chopped
4	ounces	mozzarella cheese
1	teaspoon	lemon juice
1/4	teaspoon	salt
1/4	cup	margarine
1	cup	chicken broth
8	ounces	egg noodles

Directions:
Bone, skin, and split the chicken breast in half. Cut the meat into 2 x 1/4 inch strips. Sprinkle with lemon juice, oregano, basil, salt, and pepper. Melt margarine in pan. Add chicken and onion. Cook until browned, about 5-7 minutes. Add chicken broth, reduce heat, cover, and cook 10 minutes longer. Add cheese, cover, and cook until melted. Serve over hot noodles prepared according to directions on package.

Chicken or Turkey Hash

Serves 4

Ingredients:

2	tablespoons	butter, melted or chicken fat (up to 3 teaspoons)
1		onion, thinly sliced
1/2	cup	celery, diced
2	cups	turkey or chicken, cooked, diced (up to 3 cups)

Sauce:

2	tablespoons	turkey or chicken fat, or butter
3	tablespoons	flour
2 1/2	cups	water
1/2	teaspoon	savory
1/2	teaspoon	salt
1/2	teaspoon	pepper
1/4	cup	cream

Hot biscuits:

2	cups	flour, all-purpose
1	tablespoon	baking powder
1	teaspoon	salt
3/4	cup	cream
2		eggs, beaten
3/4	cup	pickled beats

Directions:
Heat in frying pan 2-3 tablespoons of melted butter or turkey or chicken fat. Add thinly sliced onion and diced celery. Heat 5-8 minutes over low heat, stirring often. Add 2-3 cups cooked turkey or chicken.
Cook 5 minutes over low heat.
Sauce: brown the turkey or chicken fat or butter and flour well before adding water. Add savory, salt, and pepper to taste. When sauce is smooth and creamy, add 1/4 cup cream and any remaining turkey or chicken gravy. Pour over turkey. Simmer 15 minutes, then serve with hot biscuits and pickled beets.

Hot biscuits: Sift flour, baking powder and salt together in a bowl. Mix together cream with 2 beaten eggs. Add to flour and mix just enough to moisten. The dough is rather soft and should remain lumpy. Stir as little as possible. Drop by spoonfuls on a greased cookie sheet. Cook 16 minutes at 400F.

Chicken and Noodles

Courtesy of The Wheat Foods Council
Serves 8

Ingredients:

2	cups	cooked chicken, diced
6	cups	chicken broth
1	pound	frozen egg noodles or your favorite noodles
½		sweet red pepper, chopped
½		sweet green pepper, chopped
½		large onion, cut into rings
8	ounces	fresh mushrooms, sliced
or		
1	4 ounce	can mushroom slices

salt and pepper to taste

Directions:
Place chicken in a large pot with broth. Add peppers and onions. Simmer 10 minutes. Add noodles and cook according to package directions. Five minutes before noodles are done, add mushrooms. Serve hot.

Honey Roasted Chicken

Courtesy of The National Broiler Council
Serves 4

Ingredients:

1		whole broiler-fryer chicken
½	cup	water
¼	cup	honey
2	tablespoons	olive oil
½	teaspoon	curry powder
1	teaspoon	salt
½	teaspoon	pepper
1	can (16 ounces)	peach halves, drained

Directions:
Pour water into bottom of 9 x 13 inch baking pan with a roasting rack. In small saucepan, mix together honey, olive oil, and curry powder. Bring to a boil over medium temperature. This can be done in a microwave in glass measuring cup, at full power for 2 minutes.
Place chicken on rack, breast side up, and brush with honey mixture. Spoon 2 teaspoons of mixture into center cavity and sprinkle chicken with salt and pepper. Place chicken in 375F oven for 30 minutes. Remove from oven. Turn chicken over and arrange peach halves in bottom of pan, spoon pan juices over chicken and peaches and return to oven. Roast 30 minutes more, or until fork can be inserted in chicken with ease.

Mom always appreciated a little help.

Tart and Tangy Grilled Chicken

Courtesy of The National Broiler Council
Serves 4

Ingredients:

4		broiler-fryer chicken quarters
4	tablespoons	margarine
½	cup	finely chopped onion
½	cup	red wine vinegar
¼	cup	low-sodium soy sauce
¼	cup	sugarless, all-fruit orange marmalade
¾	teaspoon	salt
½	teaspoon	pepper

Directions:
In small frying pan, melt margarine over medium temperature. Add onion and cook, stirring, until clear (about 5 minutes). Stir in vinegar, soy sauce, and orange marmalade. Pour mixture into food processor or blender and blend about 1 minute.
Sprinkle chicken with salt and pepper and arrange in shallow bowl in single layer. Pour sauce over chicken, cover and refrigerate for at least 2 hours. At cooking time, place chicken on prepared grill, skin side up, about 8 inches from heat. Place marinade in small saucepan on grill or stove top and heat to boiling. Grill chicken, turning and basting with sauce every 10 minutes, for about 1 hour, or until fork can be inserted in chicken with ease.

Chicken and Potato Dumplings

Courtesy of The National Broiler Council
Serves 4

Ingredients:

1		cooked broiler-fryer chicken, skinned, boned, cut in pieces
5	cups	chicken broth, divided
5	slices	day-old whole grain bread
1¼	cups	potato, grated (about 4 small potatoes)
2	tablespoons	grated onion
2	tablespoons	grated parmesan cheese
3		eggs
1	teaspoon	seasoned salt, divided
¼	teaspoon	pepper
½	cup	flour

Directions:
Pour ½ cup of the chicken broth over bread; let soak 2-3 minutes. Drain off liquid and break bread into small, fluffy pieces. Add potato, onion, parmesan cheese, 1 of the eggs (beaten), ½ teaspoon of the seasoned salt and pepper. Mix well and shape into 2 inch rounded balls, roll in flour. Make all dumplings (about 15-20) before beginning to cook any. In dutch oven at least 10 inches in diameter, place remaining chicken broth and bring to a boil. With slotted spoon, gently place each dumpling in boiling broth. When all dumplings are arranged in broth, cover and boil about 15 minutes. Boil remaining 2 eggs until hard, and chop. Sprinkle remaining ½ teaspoon of the seasoned salt on chicken. When dumplings are done, remove to warm bowl. Add chopped egg and chicken to chicken broth. Simmer about 5 minutes. Spoon chicken and broth mixture over dumplings and serve hot.

Dorothy's Dumplings

Courtesy of The Wheat Foods Council
Serves 12

Ingredients:

1	cup	all-purpose flour
2	tablespoons	cornstarch
3	teaspoons	baking powder
½	teaspoon	salt
1		egg, beaten
½	cup	skim milk

Directions:
In a medium bowl combine flour, cornstarch, baking powder, and salt. Stir in egg and milk, mix just until the dry ingredients are moistened. Form into 12 equally sized balls of dough. Using a tablespoon, drop the dough into a boiling stew or broth. Cover tightly and boil gently 10 minutes, or until dumplings are fluffy and no longer doughy underneath. To get tender, fluffy dumplings, be sure the stew is boiling and covered constantly. Serve immediately. Makes 12 dumplings.

Dorothy's Dumplings are a great side dish with any meat.

Nothing makes your mouth water like Chicken and Potato Dumplings.

Mom's Chicken 'n' Dumplings

Serves 4

Ingredients:

4-5	pounds	cut up roasting chicken
¾	cup	sifted flour
2	tablespoons	butter or margarine
1	tablespoon	salt
½	teaspoon	pepper
1	small	white onion

boiling water

Directions:

You can use either a roasting or a fricassee chicken, but of course the roasting chicken will be better and will cook quicker. Clean the chicken, cut up, and wash thoroughly in cold water. Reserve the extra fat. Sift ¾ cup of flour into a large bowl. Place pieces of chicken into the flour and press in as much flour as possible

Before starting to cook the chicken, chop the onion very fine. Put a kettle of water on the stove to boil.

Put the chicken fat into a large pot, and put the pot over the heat to melt the chicken fat, adding the 1 tablespoon butter. Into this sizzling fat place the pieces of floured chicken, and brown both sides of each piece. Put in new pieces of chicken as the first are browned, lifting the browned pieces to a plate as the other pieces are being browned. If the pot becomes too dry add more butter as necessary.

When all the chicken is brown add the onion and let that slightly brown. Return chicken to pot and add enough boiling water to just cover the chicken, seasoning with the salt and black pepper. Allow this to just simmer, covering the pot with the lid. Simmer a roasting chicken for 2 hours. Allow a fricassee chicken to simmer longer. With a fricassee chicken, it may be necessary to add a little boiling water from time to time, if the gravy boils down.

Mom's Dumpling Recipe

Ingredients:

1½	cups	sifted flour
1½	teaspoons	salt
4	teaspoons	baking powder
½	cup	milk

Directions:

Sift together flour, baking powder, and salt mix thoroughly by stirring. Add milk slowly and mix into a heavy wet dough. Take heaping teaspoons

of dumpling dough and carefully float on top of chicken and gravy. The gravy should be heavy. If gravy is very thin, place dumplings on top of chicken. Place lid on pot and cook 15 minutes.

Roast Chicken with Potato Stuffing

Serves 4

Ingredients:

1		egg
1		roasting chicken (allow ½ pound per serving)
5	large	potatoes
2	tablespoons	chopped nuts (almonds, brazil nuts, pecans)
1	medium	onion
1	teaspoon	caraway seed
1	tablespoon	chopped parsley
1	tablespoon	melted butter or margarine

Directions:

Wash potatoes and boil them with their skins on. When done, peel and mash. Grate and add the onion to the mashed potatoes. Add the nuts and desired herbs, caraway seed, chopped parsley, melted butter, and egg. Mix all together and season to taste with salt and pepper. The chicken should be thoroughly washed before being stuffed. Also remove some of the fat.

Then stuff the chicken with this mixture. Sew the chicken up carefully where the stuffing was put in, using an in-and-over lacing stitch. It is important to sew up the opening in the chicken so that the liquid does not run in when the chicken is being basted. Before placing the chicken in the roasting pan put the roasting pan over the heat and place in it all the chicken fat that you removed. When this is melted, place the chicken in the pan and with a large spoon baste the melted fat over the chicken.

Sift some flour all over the chicken. Turn it over and sift flour on other side, then sprinkle well with salt and pepper and bake at 450F for 30 minutes. Then reduce heat to 350F and roast 20 minutes for every pound. Be sure to baste every 15 minutes.

Make a gravy when the chicken is finished roasting. Remove the chicken from the roasting pan to a large platter. Then pour the hot grease from the roasting pan into a crock, leaving only 2 tablespoonfuls

in the pan. Into these 2 tablespoons of hot fat sift 3 tablespoons of flour, stirring vigorously with a fork, until the mixture is browned. The flour must be completely mixed with the hot grease so that there are no lumps. Then pour in 3 cups of water. Place roasting pan over moderate heat and stir constantly until the gravy thickens. Stir thoroughly in order to mix in the browned juices which have solidified on the bottom of the roasting pan. This will color and flavor the gravy. Salt and pepper the gravy to taste.

Chicken Italian Style
Serves 4

Ingredients:

1		roasting chicken
3		red or green peppers
4	medium	onions
6		sliced apricots or canned, drained apricots
¾	cup	olive oil
1	can	tomatoes
3	cloves	garlic
salt and pepper		

Place half the olive oil into a frying pan which has a lid or use a baking pan with cover. Wash the chicken and cut up into small pieces. Sprinkle salt and pepper over chicken and put into the hot olive oil. Cover and simmer gently 1 ½ hours or until tender.
One half hour before chicken is done cut onions into slices and place into another frying pan with the rest of the olive oil. Cook slowly for about 15 minutes. At the same time place the tomatoes in a pot. Season to taste, add the garlic, and simmer for 30 minutes.
While the onions are cooking, remove seeds from peppers and cut into strips about 1 inch wide.
Add the peppers and apricots to the onions after the onions have cooked 15 minutes and simmer for 10 minutes. Then add the onions and peppers to the chicken and simmer for 10 more minutes. Then add the tomatoes, which should be cooked into a sauce, and serve.

Chicken In A Pot
Serves 4

Ingredients:

2		tender 3 pound chickens
1	teaspoon	salt and pepper
4	tablespoons	flour
2	slices	onion
½	pound	sliced mushrooms
1		thin slice lemon peel
4	tablespoons	butter or margarine
3	cups	water
4	tablespoons	cooking wine or juice of 1 orange

Directions:
Either a glass or earthenware casserole may be used. Heat the casserole. Cut the chickens into pieces for serving. Dust with flour, salt, and pepper. Brown the chicken in hot butter in a frying pan. Lay the meat in the hot casserole. Cook the onion, mushrooms, and lemon peel in frying pan. Add butter and stir in the flour. Add water and wine or orange juice. Salt and pepper to taste. When this has thickened pour it over the chicken in the casserole. Place in a 400F oven. When the liquid in the casserole is bubbling reduce heat to 300F and cook for 3 hours. Longer cooking will not harm this dish if it is cooked slowly.

Spicy Chicken
Serves 4

Ingredients:

2		2½ pound chickens
½	cup	butter or margarine
2	tablespoons	chopped onion
2	cups	rice
1	pinch	saffron
1		bay leaf
8	sprigs	fresh parsley
1	sprig	thyme
1½	quarts	chicken broth (6 cups)
minced parsley		
salt and pepper to taste		

Directions:
Use a Dutch oven in preparing this dish. Clean, wash, and cut up the chickens into serving pieces as for stew. Season to taste with salt and pepper and brown over moderate heat in the butter, turning the pieces frequently. When golden brown, lift out the chicken and keep hot by placing on a plate and covering with aluminum foil. Lightly brown the onion in the remaining butter in the pan. Then stir in the washed and drained rice, adding more butter if needed, so that each grain will be moistened by the butter. Stir in the saffron and mix well.
Tie together the bay leaf, fresh parsley, and thyme with white kitchen thread. Add to the rice and cook for 5 minutes, stirring occasionally.
Arrange the chicken over the rice and gently pour the chicken broth over everything. Bring to a rapid boil, stir and cover tightly. Place the pan in the oven and bake at 375 to 400F for about 25 to 30 minutes, or until the rice has absorbed all the stock or liquid. Discard the bundled spices and arrange the rice on a heated platter with the chicken on top. Dust with minced parsley. Serve immediately.

Hearty Broiled Chicken and Potatoes

Courtesy of The National Broiler Council
  Serves 4

Ingredients:

4		broiler-fryer chicken quarters
¼	cup	fresh lemon juice
6	tablespoons	parmesan cheese, divided
3	tablespoons	fresh parsley, divided
1	teaspoon	garlic salt, divided
½	teaspoon	pepper, divided
6		small potatoes, peeled
1	cup	water
½	teaspoon	salt
1		green pepper, cut in strips

Directions:

In shallow dish, mix together lemon juice, 4 tablespoons of the parmesan cheese, 2 tablespoons of the parsley, ½ teaspoon of the garlic salt, and ¼ teaspoon of the pepper. Dip chicken, one piece at a time, in mixture, dredging to coat. Set oven temperature at 450F and place rack 6 inches from heat. Arrange chicken on broiler pan and broil, turning, about 30 minutes, or until fork can be inserted in chicken with ease. Place potatoes in a small saucepan, add water and salt. Boil at medium temperature about 15 minutes, or until just before tender. Add green pepper and cook about 5 minutes more. In small bowl, mix together remaining 2 tablespoons parmesan cheese, 1 tablespoon parsley, ½ teaspoon garlic salt, and ¼ teaspoon pepper. Cut cooked potatoes and add to cheese mixture, one piece at a time, dredging to coat. Place potatoes around broiled chicken. Add pepper curls and return to broiler for 5 more minutes.

Herb Roasted Chicken

Courtesy of The National Broiler Council
  Serves 4

Ingredients:

1		whole broiler-fryer chicken
3	tablespoons	vinegar
2	tablespoons	olive oil
1	tablespoon	butter
1	tablespoon	lemon juice
1	teaspoon	seasoned salt
½	teaspoon	savory leaves
½	teaspoon	basil leaves
1	clove	garlic, minced
12	ounces	fresh mushrooms

Directions:

In small saucepan, mix together vinegar, olive oil, butter, lemon juice, seasoned salt, savory, basil, and garlic. Place over medium high heat and bring to a boil, stirring. Remove from heat, dip mushrooms in sauce and set aside. Dip whole chicken in sauce, turning to coat well. Place chicken on rack in roasting pan, breast side down. Roast in 375F oven, basting with sauce every 20 minutes, until chicken is brown and fork can be inserted with ease (about 1¼ to 1½ hours). Add mushrooms to pan during last 20 minutes of roasting time.

Hearty Broiled Chicken and Potatoes are great on a crisp fall day.

Herb Roasted Chicken is a great main dish when special guests will be stopping by.

Holiday Glazed Chicken

Courtesy of The National Broiler Council
Serves 8

Ingredients:

8		broiler-fryer chicken breast halves
½	cup	ketchup
¼	cup	white vinegar
2	tablespoons	English pub mustard
¾	teaspoon	salt
¼	teaspoon	pepper
¼	cup	butter, melted
2	tablespoons	honey

Holly Garnish ingredients:

1		green pepper
4		maraschino cherries

Directions:
Mix together ketchup, vinegar, and English pub mustard (do not substitute; this seed-filled mustard is different from salad mustard). Brush mixture over chicken; place chicken in bowl, cover and refrigerate overnight. Approximately 1 hour before serving, arrange chicken in shallow baking pan which has been sprayed with vegetable cooking spray or lined with aluminum foil. Shake off any excess sauce and add to remainder in bowl; set aside. Place chicken in 325F oven for about 45 minutes. In small saucepan mix together reserved marinating sauce, melted butter, and honey. Heat only until honey and butter mix well with sauce, about 2 minutes.
To make holly garnish: With paring knife or scissors, cut green pepper into 16 "holly leaves," split 4 maraschino cherries into halves to form "berries." On each chicken breast half, arrange 2 "holly leaves" with "berry" in center.
Brush with sauce and bake 15 minutes more, or until fork can be inserted in chicken with ease.

Chicken With Bacon

Serves 4

Ingredients:

1 or 2		split broilers or 1 cut up roasting chicken
1	cup	flour
1 or 2		eggs
1	cup	bread crumbs
1	cup	finely chopped nuts
1	cup	butter or margarine
1		thin slice broiled bacon

salt, pepper, paprika to taste

Directions:
Wash chicken thoroughly. Dry with clean damp cloth to remove any excess water, then dredge in flour. Beat eggs sufficiently to combine white and yolks, dip chicken in beaten egg and then in chopped nuts and bread crumbs. Sift a little salt, pepper, and paprika over each piece and press in. Lightly butter each piece and place in a pot. Place pot over medium heat and when it is very hot put in the slice of bacon, then put in the pieces of chicken. When the chicken is thoroughly browned on all sides, remove from fat with large fork and place on hot plates, or platter. Serve with boiled new potatoes with melted butter and finely chopped parsley and a salad of hearts of lettuce and tomatoes.

Tasty Grilled Chicken Quarters

Courtesy of The National Broiler Council
Serves 4

Ingredients:

4		broiler-fryer chicken leg-thigh quarters
¼	teaspoon	coarsely ground pepper
1	can	10½ ounces beef broth
3	tablespoons	soy sauce
1		lemon, thinly sliced
1	tablespoon	olive oil
1	tablespoon	red wine vinegar
1	tablespoon	white wine
1	clove	garlic, minced
½	teaspoon	salt

Directions:
Pat chicken quarters with pepper, rubbing into pieces. In medium bowl, mix together beef broth, soy sauce, lemon, olive oil, red wine vinegar, white wine, and garlic. In large bowl, place chicken and pour sauce over all; let marinate overnight. Place chicken on prepared grill, skin side up, about 6-8 inches from heat. Cook, turning and basting with sauce every 10 minutes for about 75 minutes, or until fork can be inserted in chicken with ease. Sprinkle salt on chicken before serving.
Add chicken and cook, turning, about 10 minutes, or until brown on all sides. Pour any remaining vinegar over chicken, reduce heat to medium low and continue to cook, turning, until chicken is done (about 20 minutes), and fork can be inserted with ease.

Baked Turkey

Serves 6

Ingredients:

1		turkey, any weight
½	cup	butter, in slices
½	cup	oil

1	teaspoon	allspice
1	teaspoon	vegetable salt or seasoning salt
4	cloves	garlic, pressed

Directions:
Preheat your oven to 400F. Place turkey in roasting pan. Lift skin above body cavity and insert butter slices. Rub oil all over skin. Sprinkle with seasonings. Cover the top of the turkey with aluminum foil and use the overlapping foil to fit around the top of the roasting pan. Cover with lid if available. Reduce heat to 350F and cook 20 minutes for every pound. Remove foil during last 20 minutes of cooking to allow skin to brown.

Mom's Favorite Thanksgiving or Holiday Turkey 'n' Gravy
Serves 12

Ingredients:

12	pound	turkey
6	tablespoons	flour
1	cup	chicken broth

salt and pepper (and paprika) to taste

Directions:
If turkey is frozen it may be defrosted in the microwave oven (follow directions in your manual), or it may be defrosted by placing it in the refrigerator overnight or until thawed.
Wash turkey and pat it dry. Sprinkle inside cavity with salt and pepper to taste. Tie legs together. Tie wings and legs to body. Invert a heat-resistant, non-metallic saucer or small casserole cover in a shallow, 10-inch, heat-resistant, non-metallic baking dish. Place turkey breast-side-down on the saucer.
Heat, uncovered, for half of cooking time (36 minutes, 3 minutes per pound). Turn the turkey breast-side-up and continue cooking, covered with a paper towel, for the remaining half of the cooking time (3 minutes per pound, or an additional 36 minutes).
Insert a meat thermometer into fleshy portion of turkey, not touching any bones. It should register 160F. Do not place thermometer in microwave oven while cooking.

If temperature is not 160F, return turkey to microwave oven for an additional few minutes until correct temperature is reached.
Let turkey stand, covered with aluminum foil, at room temperature for 20 to 30 minutes to finish cooking. The internal temperature of the turkey should be 170F after standing.
While the turkey is standing at room temperature, prepare the gravy. The turkey should be removed from the roasting pan.
Pour the pan drippings into a bowl, leaving the residue in the pan. Allow the fat to rise to the top. Skim off about 6 tablespoons of fat. Reserve pan drippings. (If there is not enough fat, add butter or margarine to make 6 tablespoons total. Discard any excess fat.)
Return fat to the baking dish. Blend in flour, salt and pepper to taste.
Heat, uncovered, in microwave oven 4 minutes, or until lightly browned.
Measure the remaining pan drippings and add enough chicken broth to make 3 cups.
Gradually stir liquid into flour mixture until smooth, scraping the sides of the pan to loosen any particles that stick to the pan.
Heat, uncovered, in microwave oven 14 minutes, or until thickened and smooth. Stir occasionally during last half of cooking.

A well-stocked fridge is a key ingredient in an efficient kitchen.

Tarragon Chicken

Courtesy of The National Broiler Council
  Serves 4

Ingredients:

4		broiler-fryer chicken leg-thigh combinations
¼	cup	flour
1	teaspoon	salt
½	teaspoon	tarragon
½	teaspoon	pepper
4	tablespoons	tarragon vinegar
3	tablespoons	olive oil

Directions:
On a piece of wax paper, mix together flour, salt, tarragon and pepper. Place vinegar in a shallow dish. Roll each piece of chicken in vinegar, then dust lightly with flour mixture. In large, non stick frying pan, place olive oil and heat over medium high temperature. Add chicken and cook, turning, about 10 minutes, or until brown on all sides. Pour any remaining vinegar over chicken, reduce heat to medium low and continue to cook, turning, until chicken is done (about 20 minutes), and fork can be inserted with ease.

Tarragon brings out the best in chicken, and the smell makes you think of Thanksgiving.

Midwest Chicken Fricassee sounds fancy, but it's really down-home good.

Midwest Chicken Fricassee

Courtesy of The National Broiler Council
Serves 4

Ingredients:

1		broiler-fryer chicken, cut in parts and skinned
½	cup	flour
1	teaspoon	paprika
1	teaspoon	chopped fresh parsley
1	teaspoon	celery salt
¼	teaspoon	freshly ground pepper
¼	cup	butter-flavored shortening
1		small onion, sliced
3	cups	chicken broth
1		bay leaf
¼	teaspoon	rosemary
8		hot baking powder biscuits

Directions:

In shallow dish, mix together flour, paprika, parsley, celery salt, and pepper. Place chicken, one piece at a time, in flour mixture, dredging to coat on all sides. Reserve 3 tablespoons of remaining flour mixture. In dutch oven, melt shortening over medium high temperature. Add chicken and cook, turning, about 10 minutes, until brown on all sides. Drain chicken on paper towels. Reduce temperature to medium, add onion and cook, stirring, about 3 minutes, or until onion is almost transparent. Add reserved 3 tablespoons of the flour mixture and continue to stir until brown, about 2 minutes. Slowly add chicken broth and bring to a boil. Boil about 2 minutes. Add bay leaf and rosemary. Return chicken to pan, reduce temperature to low, cover and cook about 30 minutes, or until fork can be inserted in chicken with ease. (Prepare biscuits while chicken cooks.) Split hot biscuits in half and serve fricassee over biscuits.

Mom'n'Pop's
Main Dishes with Meat

Old-Fashioned Meat Loaf

Serves 6

Ingredients:

1½	pounds	lean ground beef
3		bread slices or ½ cup of dry bread crumbs
1		egg, large
1	cup	milk
¼	cup	onion, chopped (1 small)
1	tablespoon	Worcestershire sauce
1	teaspoon	salt
½	teaspoon	mustard, dry
¼	teaspoon	pepper
¼	teaspoon	sage
¼	teaspoon	garlic powder
½	cup	ketchup, chili sauce or barbeque sauce as a topping.

Directions:

Heat the oven to 350F. Mix all the ingredients except the ketchup together. Spread the meat mixture into an ungreased 9 x 5 x 3 inch loaf pan, or shape into a loaf in an ungreased baking pan. Spoon ketchup onto the loaf and bake, uncovered, for 1 to 1¼ hours, or until done. Drain off the excess fat and serve sliced on a heated platter.

For leftover meat loaf, try the following:

Barbequed Meat Loaf:

For four ½ inch slices of meat loaf, mix ½ cup of barbeque sauce and 2 tablespoons of water in a skillet. Place the slices of meat loaf in the skillet, turning to coat all sides with the barbeque sauce. Cover and cook over low heat, brushing the sauce on the slices occasionally, until the meat is hot, about 10 to 15 minutes.

Potato Meat Loaf:

For four ½ inch slices of meat loaf, prepare instant mashed potatoes, enough for 4 servings, as directed on the package and set aside. Set the oven control at broil or 550F. Broil the slices with the tops 3 to 4 inches from the heat for 5 minutes. Spread the potatoes on the slices and sprinkle with shredded cheddar cheese. Broil until the cheese is melted, about 2 minutes, and serve hot.

Creamed Meat Loaf:

For four ½-inch slices of meat loaf, mix ½ to 1 can of your favorite condensed cream soup, such as cream of mushroom (10¾ ounce size) and ¼ to ½ cup of milk in a skillet. Heat to boiling, stirring frequently. Reduce the heat and place the slices in the skillet, turning to coat all sides with the sauce. Cover and simmer until the meat is hot, 10 to 15 minutes, and serve.

Grandma's Special Meat Loaf

Serves 6

Ingredients:

1½	pounds		ground meat
1½	teaspoons		salt
1	cup		bread crumbs
¼	teaspoon		pepper
8	ounces		tomato sauce with onions
		2 tablespoons	brown sugar
		2 tablespoons	mustard
		1	egg
		1 tablespoon	vinegar

Directions:

Mix meat, bread crumbs, half of the tomato sauce, egg, salt, and pepper. Shape into loaf. Combine remaining ingredients with the second half of the tomato sauce. Pour over meat. Bake at 350F for 75 minutes.

Easy Meat Loaf

Serves 6 to 8

Ingredients:

1½	pounds	ground beef
1		egg, beaten
½	cup	bread crumbs
½	cup	tomato juice
3	tablespoons	chopped onion
3	tablespoons	sliced bell pepper
3	tablespoons	chopped celery
2	teaspoons	seasoned salt
¼	teaspoon	thyme
		ketchup or chili sauce

Directions:

Using a fork, mix all the ingredients except the ketchup and pepper rings. Shape into a loaf and put into greased crock pot. Top with ketchup and pepper rings. Cover and cook on high for 1 hour, and then on low for 6 to 8 hours. Quartered potatoes coated with butter may also be cooked with this recipe. A dash of paprika will give them a nice browned look. Use the same cooking time even if you choose to add potatoes.

Mom's Meat Loaf Roast

Serves 8

Ingredients:

2	pounds	lean ground beef
½	cup	onion, chopped (1 medium)
1		egg, large
½	cup	oats, quick-cooking
½	cup	milk
1	tablespoon	parsley, snipped
1½	teaspoons	salt
½	teaspoon	savory or thyme
¼	teaspoon	pepper
½	cup	ketchup or chili sauce
2	tablespoons	brown sugar, packed

Directions:

Heat the oven to 350F. Mix all the ingredients except the ketchup and brown sugar together. Press the mixture firmly in an ungreased loaf pan measuring 8½ x 4½ x 2½ inches. Loosen the edge with a spatula and unmold the loaf into an ungreased baking pan 13 x 9 x 2 inches. Mix the ketchup and sugar and then spoon them onto the loaf. Bake uncovered for about 1 to 1¼ hours. Remove the meat loaf to a plate and let stand for 10 minutes. Then slice and serve on a heated platter. Note: If you don't have a pan this size, just form the mixture into a loaf in the large baking pan. Another variation is to press the meat mixture firmly into an ungreased 5 to 6 cup ring mold. Unmold in the baking

pan by rapping mold against the bottom of the larger pan. Brush with the ketchup mixture. Bake for about 50 minutes. If you desire, the hole in the ring can be filled with hot potato salad or creamed peas.

Horseradish Meat Loaf

Serves 12

Ingredients:

2	pounds	ground chuck or sirloin
¾	cup	oatmeal
1		onion
½	cup	ketchup
¼	cup	milk
2		eggs
4	tablespoons	horseradish
1	teaspoon	salt
¼	teaspoon	pepper
½	cup	ketchup
3	tablespoons	brown sugar
2	teaspoons	mustard (prepared)

Directions:

Combine first 9 ingredients, reserving 1 tablespoon of horseradish. Shape into two 7½ x 4 inch loaves. Place on a lightly greased rack of a broiler pan. Bake at 350F for 40 minutes. Combine ½ cup ketchup, the reserved 1 tablespoon of horseradish, and remaining ingredients. Spoon over meat loaf and bake an additional 5 minutes. Yields 2 loaves.

Cheese 'n' Meat Loaf

Serves 8

Ingredients:

1	pound	ground beef
½	tablespoon	pepper
¾	cup	cheddar cheese, cubed
½	tablespoon	celery seed
½		onion, chopped
¼	tablespoon	paprika
½		bell pepper, chopped
½	cup	milk
1		egg, beaten
½	cup	bread crumbs, dry
1	tablespoon	salt

Directions:

Preheat oven to 350F. Mix all ingredients together. Place in loaf pan. Bake for 1 hour and 15 minutes. You may find it helpful to form this in a ball and place it on a rack to cook, so that most of the fat drips away from the meat. This meat loaf makes great sandwiches and is flavorful when cold.

Rib Eye Steaks N' Seasoned Vegetable Kabobs

Courtesy of The National Cattleman's Beef Association
Serves 6

Ingredients:

3		beef rib eye steaks, cut 1 inch thick (approximately 2 pounds)
6		small (3 ounces each) red potatoes, halved
4	teaspoons	minced fresh oregano leaves, divided
¼	teaspoon	ground red pepper
2		medium yellow squash, cut into 1 inch pieces
3	tablespoons	butter or margarine, melted
1		large clove garlic, crushed

salt and pepper, as desired

Directions:
Place potatoes in 11 x 7½ inch microwave safe baking dish. Cover and microwave on high 6 to 7 minutes, or until barely fork tender, rearranging potatoes after 3 minutes. Meanwhile, combine 2 teaspoons oregano and red pepper. Sprinkle on both sides of beef rib eye steaks and reserve. Alternately thread cooked potatoes and squash on six 8 inch skewers. Combine butter, garlic and remaining 2 teaspoons oregano. Brush half of mixture over vegetables. Place steaks and kabobs on grill over medium coals. Grill steaks 9 to 12 minutes for rare to medium, turning once; grill kabobs 10 minutes, turning once and brushing with remaining butter mixture. Season steak and vegetables with salt and pepper to taste.

Note: A beef rib eye steak will yield three 3-ounce cooked, trimmed servings per pound.
The microwave variation on this recipe was tested in 650-watt microwave oven. If your oven has a different wattage, adjust times accordingly.

Mom 'n' pop always liked to have some friends over for a barbeque.

**Rib Eye Steaks N' Seasoned Vegetable Kabobs are the perfect backyard grill fare.**

Mom's Barbequed Roast

Serves 8

Ingredients:

1		four-pound beef leg, blade or rib pot roast
2	teaspoons	salt
½	teaspoon	pepper
8	small	potatoes, cut in half
8	medium	carrots, cut into quarters
8	small	onions
1	cup	barbeque sauce

Directions:

Cook beef roast in dutch oven over medium heat until brown. Reduce heat. Pour on barbeque sauce. Sprinkle with salt and pepper. Heat to boiling. Reduce heat. Cover and simmer on top of range or bake in 325F oven 2½ hours. Add vegetables. Cover and cook about 1 hour longer or until beef and vegetables are tender. Remove to warm, platter. Keep warm. Skim fat from sauce. Spoon sauce over beef and vegetables.

Cleaning up after the Barbeque.

Pop's Barbequed Ribs

Serves 4

Ingredients:

4	pounds	spareribs, cut to serve
¼	cup	ketchup
1	teaspoon	dry mustard
¼	cup	dark rum
2	cloves	garlic, crushed
1	cup	brown sugar, firmly packed
¼	cup	soy sauce
½	cup	chili sauce
¼	cup	Worcestershire sauce
1	dash	pepper

Directions:

Wrap ribs in double thickness of foil and bake for 1½ hours at 350F. Unwrap and drain drippings. Combine all remaining ingredients and pour over ribs. Marinate at room temperature for 1 hour. Bake at 350F 30 minutes, basting with sauce, or grill for 30 minutes, 4 inches above coals while periodically turning and basting.

Pop's Own Barbeque Sauce

Serves 4

Ingredients:

¾	cup	chopped onion
½	cup	lemon juice
2	teaspoons	salt
¾	cup	water
2	tablespoons	prepared mustard
¾	cup	tomato ketchup
3	tablespoons	Worcestershire sauce
½	cup	salad oil
3	tablespoons	sugar
½	teaspoon	pepper

Directions:

Cook onion in oil until soft. Add remaining ingredients. Simmer 15 minutes. Good for hamburgers, steak, chicken, oysters, or other barbeque favorites.

Rainy Day Barbequed Ribs

Serves 6

Ingredients:

3	pounds	spareribs, cut between ribs
2	cups	ketchup
1	cup	chili sauce
1	cup	chopped onions
2		cloves garlic, minced
2	tablespoons	lemon juice

2	tablespoons	lime juice
¼	cup	cider vinegar
2	tablespoons	brown sugar
1	tablespoon	soy sauce
		salt and pepper to taste

Directions:

Place all ingredients except ribs in a saucepan and bring to a boil. Simmer sauce for 30 minutes until it thickens. Place ribs in a large shallow pan and pour sauce over all. Cover with aluminum foil and bake for 1½ hours at 325F. Uncover, cool enough to skim fat from sauce, and return, uncovered, to oven. Increase heat to 450F and continue baking until ribs are browned and sauce reduced, but don't allow to dry out completely.

Grandma's Liver and Onions

Serves 3

Ingredients:

½	pound	calf or beef liver*
2		medium onions, sliced
2	tablespoons	vegetable oil
¼	teaspoon	pepper
¼	teaspoon	ground sage
2	teaspoon	soy sauce (imported, if available)
1	tablespoon	lemon juice
		chopped parsley

Directions:

Cut liver into serving pieces. Mix onions, oil, pepper, and sage in 1 quart casserole. Cover and microwave on high (100%), until onions are crisp-tender, 4 to 6 minutes. Brush liver with soy sauce. Arrange with thickest pieces in a 9 inch pie plate. Spoon onions evenly over liver. Cover tightly and microwave on high (100%) for 3 minutes. Turn pie plate one-half turn. Microwave until liver is no longer pink, 1 to 3 minutes (do not overcook). Let stand 3 minutes. (Liver will continue to cook while standing.) Sprinkle with lemon juice and parsley just before serving.

*Liver should be sliced from ¼ to ½ inch thick.

Best Beef Dumplings

Serves 6

Ingredients:

8	ounces	lean ground beef
1½	tablespoons	light soy sauce
20		round won ton wrappers
		water
		scallion fans for garnish
		radish flowers for garnish

1	tablespoon	chopped parsley
1	teaspoon	minced ginger root
1	teaspoon	cornstarch
½	teaspoon	peanut oil

Directions:

In small bowl, combine beef, soy sauce, parsley, ginger root, cornstarch, and oil. Place 10 won ton wrappers on work surface. Place 2 teaspoons of filling in center of each won ton wrapper. Moisten entire edge of won ton wrapper with water. Lift both sides of wrapper and pinch together above stuffing, gathering up edges and pleating wrappers. Pinch to seal. Continue with remaining wrappers and filling. In each of two large skillets, bring 2 cups of water to a boil. Reduce heat to medium, add dumplings, not allowing them to touch. Cover lightly and steam until dumplings are firm and wrappers are soft, 15 minutes. Serve immediately. Garnish serving platter with scallion fans and radish flowers and cook another 5 minutes.

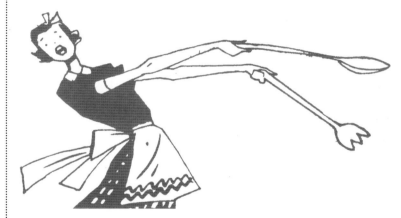

Steak 'n' Potatoes

Serves 4

Ingredients:

3	pounds	round steak, ½ inch thick
2	pounds	potatoes
8	ounces	tomato sauce
1½	teaspoons	salt
½	teaspoon	ground pepper
½	teaspoon	ground cumin
1		large clove garlic, smashed
1	cup	water

Directions:

Cut round steak into cubes and brown in shortening in heavy skillet or dutch oven. Peel and cube potatoes (approximately in ½ inch cubes). Once meat is slightly browned, add potatoes and continue to brown. (Don't worry if it sticks to the bottom of the skillet.) Add tomato sauce, salt, pepper, cumin powder, and garlic. Add approximately one cup of water and simmer until meat and potatoes are tender. Potatoes will thicken sauce.

Spicy Beef Back Ribs

Courtesy of The National Cattleman's Beef
Association
  Serves 6 to 8

Ingredients:

5	pounds	beef back ribs, cut into 3-4 rib sections
1	cup	ketchup
½	cup	water
1		medium onion, grated
2	tablespoons	fresh lemon juice
1	teaspoon	hot pepper sauce
½-1	teaspoon	crushed red pepper pods

Directions:

Combine ketchup, water, onion, lemon juice, pepper
sauce and pepper pods in small saucepan. Bring to
a boil; reduce heat. Cook slowly, uncovered, 10 to
12 minutes, stirring occasionally; keep warm.
Prepare grill for indirect cooking.* Place beef back
ribs, meat side up, on grill centered over drip pan.
Cover cooker. Grill ribs 45 to 60 minutes or until
tender, turning occasionally. Brush reserved sauce
over ribs and continue grilling, covered, 10 minutes.
*To prepare grill for indirect cooking, arrange equal
amount of briquets on each side of grill. Place
aluminum foil drip pan in center between coals.
Coals are ready when ash-covered, about 30
minutes. Make sure coals are burning equally on
both sides.
Continue grilling 10 to 20 minutes, turning once.
Brush sauce over ribs; continue cooking 10 minutes.
*To check temperature, cautiously hold hand about
4 inches above coals. Low to medium coals will
force removal of hand in 4 to 5 seconds.

Cooking out was definitely not "roughing it."

Spicy Beef Back Ribs are wonderful on the grill.

Old-Fashioned Prime Rib

Serves 8

Ingredients:

1		standing roast of beef (4-rib, about 10-11 pounds)
2	tablespoons	unflavored cooking oil
salt and pepper to taste		

Directions:
Preheat oven to 450F. Trim the excess fat from the roast, leaving only ¼-inch of fat. Heat the oil in a large roasting pan over medium-to-high heat on top of the stove. When the oil is hot, place the roast, fat-side down, in the pan and brown for 5 minutes. Turn the roast on one end and cook another 5 minutes. Turn on the other end and cook 5 minutes. Remove from heat and discard fat. Sprinkle with desired salt and pepper. Place roast in oven and immediately reduce heat to 350F. Roast approximately 12 minutes per pound for medium-rare, or about 2 hours for a 10-pound roast. Remove the pan from the oven. Remove the roast from the pan and let stand for 25 minutes before carving. To serve, strain the gravy into a sauce boat and carve the roast at the table, counting on about 2 people per rib.

Freezing the roast: Do not carve the entire roast if you don't have to. A whole solid piece of meat is more successfully cooked when defrosted than a few smaller pieces. Before freezing, heat a dry fry pan over high heat on top of the stove. Place the remainder of the roast, cut side down, in the pan and sear well. Allow the roast to cool to room temperature. Wrap with freezer paper and then cover in plastic wrap. Label and place in the freezer for up to 1 month. Defrost, without unwrapping, in the refrigerator for 24 to 28 hours. To reheat defrosted rib roast, wrap prime rib in 1 layer of microwave plastic wrap and place in a covered roasting pan or dutch oven. Cover, place in the oven, turn temperature to 250F and cook about 8 minutes per pound, or until a meat thermometer placed in the thickest part of the roast reads 110F. Remove pan from the oven and turn temperature to 450F. Unwrap the roast, replace uncovered in the pan, and replace in the oven for about 15 minutes to crust the outside.

Pork Chops in Cream Gravy

Serves 6

Ingredients:

6		loin pork chops
1		beef bouillon cube
½	cup	water
2	tablespoons	flour
2	tablespoons	brown sugar
¼	cup	water
2	tablespoons	finely chopped onion
½	cup	dairy sour cream
2	tablespoons	ketchup
1		garlic clove, minced

Directions:
In a large skillet, brown pork chops. Add ½ cup water, brown sugar, onion, ketchup, garlic, and bouillon cube. Cover. Simmer for 30-40 minutes or until tender. Remove chops to serving platter. Keep warm. In a small bowl, combine flour with ¼ cup water. Slowly add to cooking liquid, stirring constantly. Cook until thickened. Stir in sour cream. Heat thoroughly. Do not boil. Serve sauce over chops.

Pork Chops with Cheese

Serves 6

Ingredients:

6		pork chops
¼	cup	flour
		salt
		paprika
		pepper
		butter or margarine to fry in
¾	cup	milk
8	ounce pack	cream cheese, cubed
½	tablespoon	garlic salt
½	cup	parmesan cheese

Directions:
Coat the chops with the seasoned flour, and brown in margarine or butter. Heat milk and add cream cheese, garlic salt and ¼ cup parmesan cheese, mixing well until blended. Place chops in baking dish (12 x 8 inches). Cover with sauce and add remaining ¼ parmesan cheese. Bake at 325F for 50 minutes, or until chops are tender.

Barbequed Lamb Chops
Serves 4

Ingredients:

1	cup	red currant jelly
1	cup	mustard
1		rack of lamb
1	cup	white wine
½	cup	butter
½	cup	shallots, minced
2	tablespoons	rosemary, crushed

Directions:
Mix jelly and mustard in saucepan and simmer on stovetop for 5 minutes to melt jelly. Remove lamb chops from rack and french cut, being careful not to remove the fat from the eye. (The fat will protect the meat from burning on the grill.) Allow sauce to cool completely. Submerge lamb chops in sauce and allow to marinate overnight (place in refrigerator). Grill over hickory coals 4 to 5 minutes (for medium to medium-rare), basting with sauce as it cooks. Turn once half-way through cooking time. Prepare garnish sauce by browning shallots in butter and stirring in the white wine and rosemary. Serve lamb with garnish sauce and grilled potatoes and vegetables.
Note: The marinade sauce also goes well with other foods, including mushrooms.

Pop was always glad to supervise.

Grandma's Lamb Roast
Serves 4

Ingredients:

1		leg lamb
¾	cup	sifted flour
1	small	sliced onion or clove garlic
salt and pepper to taste		

Directions:
Wash lamb and place in roasting pan. Then sift flour all over it. Some of the sifted flour will go into the baking pan, but that will dissolve when you add the water. Sprinkle well with salt and pepper and then pour cold water into the baking pan until it is about 1 inch deep. On top of the roast place slices of onion. For a slight taste of garlic, use a knife to cut 5 or 6 deep holes in the top of the lamb and push one small piece of garlic, the size of a pin, into each hole.
When placing the leg of lamb in the roasting pan, place it with rounded side of the meat up. The bone part of the meat should be down and the knuckle part of the meat should be up. Potatoes will take the same time to roast as the meat. Peel the potatoes, rub with salt, and place in water around roast. Turn when brown. Place the roast in the center of a hot oven and bake at 450F for

30 minutes and then reduce heat to 325F for balance of time. Roast 25 to 30 minutes per pound.
Do not baste the roast for the first half hour, but after that baste it about every 15 minutes. Have a kettle of water boiling on the stove and if the water in the roast boils away, pour in a little boiling water. During the last half hour the roast is cooking, turn it over and let the other side brown. Turn it back over 5 minutes before taking it out of the oven. The turning of the roast will help to color your gravy and soften up the meat. You will also find when your roast is ready to serve that you have plenty of rich gravy already made.

Basic Lamb Pot Roast
Serves 4

Ingredients:

4	pounds	lamb shoulder
2	tablespoons	butter or margarine
2		sliced tomatoes
1	cup	celery
4		minced carrots
2		onions, sliced
1		thin slice garlic
2	cups	water
2	tablespoons	flour

Directions:
Have the butcher bone the lamb and remove every trace of fat. Have the meat rolled and bound in a compact mass. Brown it in butter until a rich, deep brown. Place in a kettle. Surround this with the vegetables. Add the water to the pan the meat was browned in. Pour over the vegetables. Add more hot water if necessary. The water should half cover the pot roast. Cook slowly for 2 hours. Remove the meat. Make a sauce of the vegetables and liquid in the pan by adding the flour mixed with 4 tablespoons of water. Serve with eggplant.

Oven Braised Lamb Shanks

Courtesy of The American Lamb Council
　Serves 4-6

Ingredients:

4		lamb shanks (about 1 pound each)
2	tablespoons	oil
1	cup	chopped onions
1	medium	green pepper, chopped
2	cloves	garlic, crushed
1	can (16 ounces)	tomato sauce
1	tablespoon	sugar
2	tablespoons	vinegar
1	tablespoon	grated lemon rind
¼	cup	stock or bouillon

Directions:

Heat oil to medium and add lamb shanks; cook over medium heat until browned on all sides. Remove lamb. Add onions, green pepper, and garlic. Cook for 3 minutes. Add remaining ingredients; mix well. Cook over low heat for about 10 minutes. Place lamb in 2½ quart casserole dish. Top with tomato sauce mixture. Cover with foil and bake in 325F oven for 1 hour, or until lamb shanks are tender.

We always enjoyed Oven Braised Lamb Shanks.

Glazed Leg of Lamb was always one of pop's favorite Sunday dinners.

Glazed Leg of Lamb

Courtesy of The American Lamb Council
Serves 4

Ingredients:

½		leg of lamb, sirloin end (about 4½ pounds)
½	teaspoon	salt
¼	teaspoon	thyme
¼	teaspoon	lemon pepper
½	cup	corn syrup or honey
¼	cup	red wine vinegar
2	tablespoons	ketchup

Directions:

Place lamb, fat side up, in shallow roasting pan. Sprinkle with salt, thyme, and lemon pepper. Rub seasonings into lamb surface.

In small bowl stir together corn syrup or honey, red wine vinegar, and ketchup until smooth. Use to baste lamb the last 30 minutes of roasting. Roast lamb in preheated 325F oven for 20 minutes per pound, or until meat thermometer registers 140F for rare, 150F for medium-rare.

Mom's Special Veal Cutlets

Serves 6

Ingredients:

6		veal cutlets
1	teaspoon	salt
¼	teaspoon	pepper
1	½ cups	cracker crumbs
1		slightly beaten egg
1	tablespoon	milk
½	cup	hot water
2	tablespoons	lemon juice
1		sliced hard boiled egg
6		lemon slices
2	tablespoons	capers

Directions:

Sprinkle veal with salt and pepper and pound well. Dip in crumbs, then in egg to which milk has been added, then in crumbs again and brown well in deep fat.

Place in covered baking dish with hot water and cook in 400F oven for 30 minutes. Sprinkle with lemon juice and serve garnished with hard boiled egg, lemon, and capers.

Grandma's Stuffed Lamb

Serves 4

Ingredients:

2		small or 1 large eggplant
1	pound	stewing lamb
1	medium	onion
¾	cup	rice
½	cup	seedless raisins
¼	cup	pine nuts
2	tablespoons	butter or margarine
¼	cup	flour

salt and pepper to taste

Directions:

Cut lamb in pieces, sprinkle with salt, sift flour over each piece and press it in. Place the butter (or other fat, if you prefer) in frying pan and when sizzling hot add the lamb and brown on each side. Then add enough water to completely cover the lamb, adding the onion, salt and pepper to taste and slowly simmer 30 minutes.

Meanwhile, boil the rice and prepare the eggplant. Boil about 2 quarts of water in a large pot with 2 level tablespoons of salt. Wash rice thoroughly in cold water, then drain and sprinkle into the rapidly boiling salted water.

Cook uncovered until the rice is tender. In the meantime, prepare the eggplant. Remove the stem and cut off a small part of the eggplant and with a teaspoon dig out the inside, leaving a shell about 1 inch to 1 ¼ inches thick. To prepare the stuffing, cut up some of the cooked

Fred MacMurray, the ideal 1950s pop in My Three Sons.

lamb into little pieces, until you have a cupful. It is better to use as little of the fat as possible. Pour the remainder of the meat and gravy into a large pot that has a lid. The pot should be just large enough to enable you to boil the eggplant in the stew gravy when it is stuffed. Allow the balance of the stew or liquid to continue slowly simmering.

Next, strain the water from the rice (it should be tender) and run plenty of cold water over it to remove the excess starch. Then put into a bowl the rice, cooked lamb, raisins, and pine nuts. Mix these ingredients together and salt and pepper to taste. It is important that you season well as some of the seasoning will go into the eggplant, which is not seasoned otherwise. Pack the stuffing into the eggplant as tightly as possible. Place the stuffed eggplant into the pot with the boiling stew; there should be enough liquid to float the eggplant (it won't sink all the way into the liquid, but float). If necessary, add boiling water and season to taste. Cover the pot and allow to boil very slowly until the eggplant is very soft when tested with a fork. Serve without any other vegetable. Carve across the eggplant, cutting and serving it in thick slices. This is a very delicious and unusual dish and is quite easy to prepare.

The liquid that is left can be served the following day as a soup. If there is any meat left, cut it into small pieces. If any stuffing material is left over, add it; if not, add a little rice and allow it to cook until quite soft and tender. The extra eggplant that was dug out can be fried or baked in a little butter and added to the soup. A little tomato can be added, if desired. Chill the liquid and remove the fat from the top. Reheat and serve.

Old-Fashioned Pot Roast

Serves 6

Ingredients:

5	pounds	round or pot roast
2	tablespoons	shortening
½	cup	apple cider
8		carrots, peeled and sliced
6	large	potatoes, peeled and cubed
8	ounces	fresh okra (or 10 ounces frozen)
2	teaspoons	salt
½	cup	barbeque sauce (your choice)
2		onions, sliced

Directions:

Rub meat with salt. Melt shortening in dutch oven. Add meat and cook over medium heat, turning once. Reduce heat. Pour barbeque sauce and cider over meat. Cover and simmer on top of range or in 325F oven for 3 to 4 hours. Add carrots, potatoes, and onions 1½ hours before end of cooking time. Add okra 15 minutes before end of cooking time.

Home-Style Lamb Roast

Serves 4

Ingredients:

1½	pounds	lamb steak
1	cup	vinegar
1½	cups	water
3	bay	leaves
1½	teaspoons	salt
1½	teaspoons	sugar
2	medium	yellow or red onions
1	clove	garlic, or few thin slices
6		tomatoes or 18 cherry tomatoes
1	bunch	scallions (spring onions)
1		lemon

Directions:

Pour vinegar and water into a saucepan (there should be slightly more water than vinegar). Add 3 bay leaves and the salt and sugar. Bring the mixture to the boiling point and allow to very slowly boil for about 5 minutes; then cool.

Next cut the meat into small squares, not more than 1 inch square. Slice the onions and cut the garlic into halves. If you do not have a small clove, then use 2 or 3 thin slices cut from a larger clove.

Place the meat, the onion, and the garlic into the cold vinegar and water. There should be enough of the vinegar and water to just cover the meat. Place in refrigerator and allow to soak in this mixture for 24 hours, or until ready to cook.

Remove meat from liquid and allow to drain. Cut tomatoes into thick slices and sprinkle a little salt and pepper on them, but not on the meat, which has been seasoned in the vinegar mixture. Use the cherry tomatoes whole. Using the regular 5- or 6-inch long wire meat skewers, put on a piece of meat, a slice of tomato, another piece of meat and so on, alternating with meat and slices of tomato until the skewers are filled. When placing the meat on the skewers, place all fat on the same side. When you broil these under the flame or over a heat, the fat should be on top, so that as it melts, it trickles down over the broiling meat, moistening and flavoring it.

Broil over a hot heat or under a fast flame for about 15 to 20 minutes, according to how well done you like the meat. Broil on one side and then turn when first side is browned.

Push the meat and tomatoes off the skewers onto the plates and put a quarter lemon on each plate. The lemon should be squeezed over the meat before eating. Serve with one bunch of scallions (spring onions) that have been cut up fine; cut up the white and a part of the green. Serve no other vegetable.

Jane Wyatt, the ideal 1950s mom in Father Knows Best.

Goulash with Veal

Serves 4

Ingredients:

2	pounds	leg of veal
4	tablespoons	butter or margarine
1	large	tomato
3	large	onions
1	cup	chopped celery
1	ounce	capers (Use the capers and the liquid)
2	tablespoons	paprika
1	cup	sour cream
salt and pepper to taste		

Directions:

First prepare the ingredients. Chop onions into fairly small pieces. Cut the veal into very small squares. Put the butter into a large saucepan, or a frying pan which has a close fitting lid and place saucepan over moderate heat. When butter is hot, put in the chopped onion and allow to cook until a golden brown color. Then add the veal, salt, pepper, and paprika.

Continue to cook until the meat browns. Keep turning the onion and meat over every few minutes to prevent burning. When brown add tomato and celery, cut up, and two tablespoons of water.

Cover and cook slowly for 45 minutes, adding about one tablespoon of water from time to time as necessary. When all has cooked for 45 minutes, add the capers and sour cream and allow to cook for a few minutes, then serve with fine noodles or dumplings.

Easy Pork Spareribs

Serves 2

Ingredients:

1	pound	pork spareribs cut into pieces
2		potatoes peeled and cubed
½	cup	onion slices
1	tablespoon	sherry
3	tablespoons	oyster sauce
2	tablespoons	soy sauce
½	teaspoon	sugar
2	teaspoons	oil, butter

Directions:

Lightly brown spareribs in hot skillet. Add oil, potatoes, onion, and sherry and cook 5 to 10 minutes, or until potatoes and onion are lightly browned. Mix in oyster sauce, soy sauce, and sugar and simmer 20 to 30 minutes.

Mom's Easy Do-It-Yourself Pot Roast

Serves 6

Ingredients:

2	pounds	beef roast
6		potatoes halved (not peeled)
3		onions, peeled and quartered
4		carrots, cut into 2 inch lengths
½	cup	water

Directions:

Put the vegetables on the bottom of the pot, and the meat on top. Season meat with salt and pepper. Pour water over all. Simmer all of the above on low all day. Add an envelope of onion soup mix or a small can of whole tomatoes for a variation.

Pop's Dark Beer Pot Roast

Serves 6

Ingredients:

2	pounds	beef pot roast
1	tablespoon	oil
1		diced onion
1	cup	thinly sliced carrots
3	cups	dark beer
2	cups	chicken stock
1	teaspoon	salt
1	cup	frozen peas, defrosted

Directions:

Heat oil in a pot. Add the meat and brown well on both sides. Remove the meat and pour out the fat. Replace the meat and add onion, carrot and dark beer. Place over medium heat and cook 5 minutes. Add stock and salt. Cover and cook for 1¼ hours, or until meat is tender. Add the peas and cook for another 5 minutes.

Preparing a wonderful, mouth-watering, beef pot roast.

Oven Roasted Lamb Rib Chops with Rosemary Apple Dressing

Courtesy of The American Lamb Council
  Serves 4

Ingredients:

3	tablespoons	olive oil, divided
½	cup	chopped onion
2		cloves garlic, minced
2	teaspoons	dried rosemary leaves, crushed
½	teaspoon	salt
½	teaspoon	pepper
½	cup	finely diced red bell pepper
2	cups	corn bread stuffing, crumbled
½	cup	canned apple pie filling and topping, chopped
½	cup	apple juice
1	cup	chopped walnuts
8		lean fresh lamb rib chops, cut ¾ inch thick

Directions:

In large skillet, heat 1 tablespoon olive oil and sauté onion, garlic, rosemary, salt, and pepper for 3 minutes, stirring occasionally. Add red bell pepper, corn bread stuffing, apple pie filling, apple juice, and walnuts, mixing well. Using 13 x 9 x 2 inch heat resistant baking dish, spread out dressing; set aside. In large skillet heat remaining oil and quickly brown lamb chops on each side; do not cook.
Place lamb chops on top of dressing.

Roast in preheated 350F oven for:
  20-24 minutes for rare, 140F.
  25-29 minutes for medium, 150F.
  30-34 minutes for medium well, 160F.
Serve dressing on plate and top with 2 lamb rib chops.

Oven Roasted Lamb Rib Chops with Rosemary Apple Dressing is for special occasions.

Brandied Liver and Onions

Serves 6 to 8

Ingredients:

2	tablespoons	all-purpose flour
¼	teaspoon	pepper
1	pinch	salt
1	pound	calves' liver, sliced thin
1		onion, sliced into rings
½	cup	raisins
2	tablespoons	brandy
1	tablespoon	cider vinegar

bacon as desired

Directions:

On sheet of wax paper, combine flour, pepper, and salt. Dredge liver in flour mixture. In large non-stick skillet, over medium heat, cook bacon until crisp. Remove to paper towel to drain. Crumble when cool. Add liver to drippings in pan and sauté, in batches if necessary, until golden brown (about 1½ minutes per side). Remove to serving platter. Keep warm. Add onion to skillet. Cook until soft. Stir in raisins, brandy, and cider vinegar. Cook 1 minute. Add crumbled bacon. Pour over liver.

Cold Day Beef Dish

Serves 4

Ingredients:

3	pounds	pot roast
2	tablespoons	salt
1	teaspoon	black pepper
1	bundle	carrots
1	bundle	white turnips
4		leeks (more if preferred)
		parsley
1	cup	fresh or frozen peas

Directions:

Place beef in large kettle and add four quarts of cold water. Bring to a boil and skim the top of the water. Continue to skim off any scum until it ceases to form. Then add 2 tablespoons of salt and 1 teaspoon of black pepper. Prepare the leeks by taking off the outside layer and cutting off about ½ of the length of green, leaving the remainder of leeks whole. Chop up the rest of the green sections. Clean and cut up the other vegetables. Add the leeks and all the vegetables except the peas. Add the parsley and allow all to slowly simmer for 1 ¾ hours. Add the peas and continue to simmer for another 15 minutes. Then take the beef out and allow it to chill. (The roast can be eaten hot if preferred.) You will notice that the beef will swell up to more than twice the size that it was in the raw state.

When you take the meat out of the soup, remove the soup pot from the heat and reheat the soup when you are ready to serve the meat. The beef is eaten cold, with hot vegetables, including the leeks. Some of the vegetables can be cut up small and left in the soup and others left in larger pieces and served with the meat course.

Mom's Bacon 'n' Beef Ragout

Serves 4

Ingredients:

4	medium	potatoes
2	medium	carrots
3	medium	onions
1	pound	round steak
½	pound	sliced Canadian style bacon
1	cup	cold water

salt and pepper to taste

Directions:

This dinner is cooked over a single burner. Prepare in a baking pan, large saucepan, or skillet with a lid. It is important to have a lid that fits the utensil.

Wash, peel, and thinly slice the potatoes. Wash, scrape, and slice the carrots. Peel and slice the onions. Cut the round steak across the grain into little strips about 2 inches long and half an inch wide. (First stretch the meat and see which way the grain runs. Then cut across the grain. If meat is cut with the grain, it will have long, stringy pieces and it will be tough. If cut across the grain, the meat will be tender.) If ordinary bacon is used, halve the slices. Next place all the ingredients in the cooking utensil as follows:

First put the bacon in, spreading it over the bottom of the pan. Then distribute the steak in a layer over the bacon and sprinkle a little black pepper over it. Put in a layer of onions and carrots and sprinkle with a little salt and pepper. On top of all put the thinly sliced potatoes and sprinkle with a little salt and pepper. Put the pan over the heat and start cooking. After 3 minutes add the cup of water and put on the lid. Cook for 45 minutes over a very low heat, at which time water will have cooked into the ingredients.

German-style Marinated Beef

Serves 4:

Ingredients:

beef (cross rib of beef, top sirloin or bottom round, allowing ½ pound for each serving)

1	cup	cider vinegar, claret or beer
1	tablespoon	salt
2	tablespoons	sugar
12		cloves
6		bay leaves
2	medium	onions
½		sliced lemon
1	cup	blackberries or raspberries

Directions for marinating the meat:
Place meat in crock or bowl sufficiently large to allow it to be covered with liquid. Next pour in a liquid consisting of the following mixture: either half vinegar and half water, or, if you are using cooking claret, two parts claret to one part water. Dark beer such as Oktoberfest-style may also be used. Add enough to just cover the meat. Then add all the other ingredients. Leave the meat in this mixture overnight, turning once in a while.

Directions for cooking:

3	tablespoons	butter or margarine
6		ginger snaps
¾	cup	sifted flour
1	cup	cold water

Use a Dutch oven or a large pot with a tight lid. Take meat out of liquid and let drain. Reserve liquid. Place the butter in the pot and heat until sizzling. Place meat in pot and brown all over as you would for a pot roast. Then gradually add all of the reserved liquid. Add the ginger snaps and cover the pot and allow the meat to simmer slowly for 2 or 3 hours, according to the size of the meat. Just before the meat is done, place the flour on a pie pan, distributing evenly, and place in the oven at 350F to brown. When the flour is brown, add one cup of cold water. Mix thoroughly with the browned flour and pour into the pot with the meat. Cook for 10 minutes over moderate heat. If the gravy is too thick, add a little more water.
After cooking, remove the meat, strain the gravy, and put everything back in the pot, simmering for another 5 minutes before serving.

Basic Simple Beef Roast

Serves 4

Ingredients:

1		beef roast (allowing ½ pound per serving)
1	tablespoon	flour
½	cup	Worcestershire sauce (optional)

salt, pepper and/or herbs and spices to taste

Directions:
In preparing beef for roasting use no water in the pan. Rub roast with the salt, pepper, herbs and spices. Place it in a pan and bake it at 500F for 20 to 30 minutes, or until lightly browned. It has been traditionally believed that such a hot oven sears the meat, thus preventing the escape of juices.
After the meat is seared, or lightly browned, reduce the oven temperature to 300F.
Roasts of beef weighing 5 pounds or over require approximately 10 minutes to the pound to be rare, 15 minutes to the pound to be medium and 20 minutes to the pound to be well done. In addition to the weight, consideration should also be given to the thickness of the meat in determining how long it should be cooked. Baste meat with its own drippings about every 15 minutes.
To make the gravy, remove beef and pour most of the hot drippings or fat into a crock, leaving only about a tablespoon in the pan. Into this hot fat stir the flour briskly with a fork so that there are no lumps, then add water and boil for 2 or 3 minutes, stirring constantly. The juices which have been browned on the bottom of the roasting pan will dissolve, flavoring and coloring your gravy. Season gravy with salt and pepper and perhaps a very little Worcestershire sauce.

Baked Ham with Mangos

Serves 4

Ingredients:

2	large	thin slices raw or smoked ham (¼ to ½ inch thick)
1	teaspoon	dry mustard
2	teaspoons	vinegar
1		mango
½	cup	brown sugar
½	cup	butter or margarine

Directions:
Mix together the mustard and vinegar. Spread the mixture thinly on the ham. Peel, remove pit, and slice mango very thin, spreading 2 layers of the thin slices on ham. Sprinkle well with brown sugar. Next roll the ham the long way, starting from the fat side and rolling the fat into the center.
Hold together with metal butcher skewers. Place in baking pan and put a few dabs of butter on each ham roll. Bake at 375F for 25 minutes. Baste 2 or 3 times while baking.

Mom'n'Pop's
Desserts, Pies and Cookies

Party Time Angel Food Cake

Serves 6 to 8

Ingredients:

1		angel food cake
1	cup	pineapple, diced
1	cup	coconut
		or
1	cup	cherries
		or
1	cup	strawberries
1	cup	double cream, whipped
½	pound	marshmallows, cut
1	cup	pecan meats, salted

Directions:

With two forks carefully remove inside of cake, leaving firm shell. Tear the inside of the cake which you removed into small pieces and blend with whipped cream, coconut, pineapple, and cut marshmallows. Fill ring and allow to stand for several hours. When ready to serve, add more whipped cream and sprinkle with berries and salted nuts.

Easy Coffee Cake

Makes 1 loaf

Ingredients:

2	tablespoons	fat
2	tablespoons	peanut butter
¾	cup	sugar
¾	teaspoon	salt
2	teaspoons	cinnamon
1	cup	flour
1		egg

1	cup	milk, sour
1	cup	flour, sifted
½	teaspoon	baking soda
1	teaspoon	baking powder
½	cup	currants or raisins

Directions:

Mix fat and peanut butter with sugar until smooth. Sift together flour, salt, and cinnamon. Mix with peanut butter and sugar until crumbly.

Reserve ¼ cup of mixture. Beat egg and add milk, baking soda, and baking powder mixed with second cup of flour. Combine with mixture. Add floured currants or raisins. Put in greased and floured baking pan. Cover with the ¼ cup of crumbs. Bake in 375F oven for 30 minutes.

Mom's Special Coffee Cake

Serves 6

Ingredients:

4½	cups	flour
4	teaspoons	baking powder
1	teaspoon	salt
4	tablespoons	sugar
2	tablespoons	butter
2		eggs
1½	cups	milk

Topping:

1	teaspoon	cinnamon
1	tablespoon	butter
½	cup	flour
½	cup	sugar

Pop was always thrilled when sis baked him a cake.

Mom had style, whether it was in decorating the kitchen or in decorating her cakes.

Directions:

Sift flour. Add baking powder, salt, and sugar. Sift three times. Chop butter in with spoon. Beat egg whites until stiff. Add egg yolks and beat. Add milk. Beat all together. Place in 2 square pans and spread with the topping mixture.

Honey Graham Roll-up

Serves 6

Ingredients:

½	pound	honey graham crackers
½	pound	dates, pitted and chopped
½	cup	chopped nuts
½	pound	marshmallows, diced
3	tablespoons	lemon juice
¼	teaspoon	salt

Directions:

Roll crackers with a rolling pin until crumbled fine. Combine ingredients. Mix thoroughly. Add cream if too dry. Form in roll. Wrap in waxed paper. Let stand overnight. Slice. Serve with whipped cream.

Marshmallow Sauce for the Honey Graham Roll-up

Serves 12

Ingredients:

½	cup	sugar
¼	cup	water
3	tablespoons	light corn syrup
2	cups	miniature marshmallows
¾	teaspoon	vanilla
		dash of salt

Directions:

Heat sugar, water, and corn syrup to boiling in 2 quart saucepan. Reduce heat. Simmer, uncovered, 4 minutes, stirring occasionally. Remove from heat. Stir in remaining ingredients until marshmallows are melted and mixture is smooth. Makes 1½ cups of sauce. You may substitute 20 large marshmallows, cut into quarters.

Mom's Date Nut Bread

Makes 1 loaf

Ingredients:

2	cups	whole wheat pastry flour
2	teaspoons	baking powder
1	teaspoon	nutmeg
¼	cup	butter
¼	cup	maple syrup
2		eggs
2	teaspoons	vanilla
½	cup	milk
1	cup	dates, chopped
½	cup	walnuts (or other nuts), chopped

Directions:

Sift together flour, baking powder, and nutmeg. Set aside. Cream butter with maple syrup. Add eggs, vanilla, and milk. Stir in flour mixture. Fold in dates and nuts. Pour mixture into lightly buttered 9 inch x 5 inch loaf pan. Bake at 325F for 1¼ hours, or until top splits or toothpick comes out clean.

Grandma's Favorite Banana Bread

Makes 1 loaf

Ingredients:

½	cup	butter
1	cup	sugar
2		eggs, beaten
4		bananas, finely crushed
1	teaspoon	lemon juice
1½	cups	flour
1½	teaspoons	baking powder
½	teaspoon	salt
1	teaspoon	vanilla

Directions:

Cream together butter and sugar. Mash bananas. Add lemon juice to mashed bananas. Beat eggs. Add eggs and crushed bananas to the creamed butter and sugar. Combine well. Sift together flour, baking powder, and salt. Add to creamed mixture. Add vanilla. Pour into greased loaf pan. Bake at 350F for 60 minutes. Keeps well if refrigerated.

Mom's Banana-Nut Bread

Makes 2 loaves

Ingredients:

4¾	cups	all purpose flour

¾	cup	sugar
1	teaspoon	salt
2	packages	active dry yeast
½	cup	evaporated milk, undiluted
½	cup	water
½	cup	margarine
2		eggs, at room temperature
1	cup	banana, mashed
½	cup	pecans, chopped
2	teaspoons	cinnamon, ground
2	tablespoons	margarine, melted

Directions:

In large bowl, mix 1¼ cups flour, ½ cup sugar, salt, and undissolved yeast. Heat evaporated milk, water, and margarine to 120F -130F. Margarine need not melt. Add to dry ingredients. Beat 2 minutes at medium speed of mixer. Add eggs, banana, and 1 cup flour. Beat at high speed for 2 minutes. Stir in pecans and enough remaining flour to make stiff dough. Knead 8 to 10 minutes. Set in greased bowl. Grease top. Cover. Let rise until doubled, about 1 hour. Punch dough down. Divide in half. Shape into loaves. Place in 2 greased 8½ x 4½ x 2½ inch loaf pans. Cover. Let rise until doubled, about 1 hour. Mix remaining sugar and cinnamon. Brush loaves with melted margarine. Top with sugar mixture. Bake at 375F for 25 to 35 minutes. Cool.

Easy Banana Bread

Makes 1 loaf

Ingredients:

½	cup	butter
1	cup	sugar
2		eggs, beaten
4		bananas, finely crushed
1½	cups	flour
1	teaspoon	baking soda
½	teaspoon	salt
½	teaspoon	vanilla

Directions:

Cream together butter and sugar. Add eggs and crushed bananas. Combine well. Sift together flour, baking soda, and salt. Add to creamed mixture. Add vanilla. Pour into greased and floured loaf pan. Bake at 350F for 60 minutes. Keeps well if refrigerated.

Home-Style Bread Pudding

Serves 4

Ingredients:

6		slices of bread
3		eggs
2	cups	warm milk

½	cup	sugar
1	teaspoon	vanilla
½	cup	raisins
1	container	warm maple syrup on the side

Directions:

Preheat your oven to 325F. Butter a deep dish, a 9 inch pie plate or a 9 inch square cake pan. Generously butter one side of bread. Cut in half to make two triangles. Repeat with all slices. Arrange triangles, buttered side up, in prepared dish. In bowl, beat eggs until well mixed. Add milk, sugar and vanilla. Beat together. Stir in raisins. Slowly pour over bread, making sure all bread is well soaked. Bake 45 minutes, or until custard has set. Serve with warm maple syrup.

Holiday Candy Apples

Serves 6

Ingredients:

6		wooden skewers or ice cream sticks
6	medium	apples (preferably a sweet apple)
2	tablespoons	water
1	package	(14 ounces) vanilla caramels

Directions:

Insert skewer in stem end of each apple. Heat water and caramels over low heat, stirring occasionally, until caramels are melted and mixture is smooth. Keep mixture over very low heat. Dip each apple into caramel mixture, spooning mixture over apple until completely coated. Place on waxed paper. Refrigerate until coating is firm.

To microwave: Prepare apples as directed. Place water and caramels in 4-quart microwavable container. Microwave uncovered on high 3 to 4 minutes, stirring after 2 minutes, until caramels can be stirred smooth. Continue as directed. (If mixture thickens, microwave on high about 30 seconds.)

Mom's Apple Slice Bake

Serves 4

Ingredients:

4		baking apples (such as Rome apples)
½	cup	brown sugar
½	teaspoon	powdered cloves
½	teaspoon	cinnamon
½	cup	honey
½	cup	water

Directions:

Preheat your oven to 400F. Core and slice apples into ½ inch thick rings. Place in shallow baking dish. In saucepan, combine and heat remaining ingredients. Pour over apples and bake 15 minutes or until tender, turning to baste once or twice. Variation: Very good with Red-Hot candy put in the center of each ring.

Grandma's Stewed Apples

Serves 6

Ingredients:

2	pounds	apples
2	tablespoons	butter
½	cup	sugar
½	cup	water
½	cup	white wine
1	small	piece lemon peel
1	tablespoon	lemon juice

Directions:

Peel and core the apples. Cut in thick slices. Sauté in butter for 2 or 3 minutes. Sprinkle with sugar. Add water, wine, lemon peel, and lemon juice. Cover and cook slowly, until the apples are tender.

Favorite Baked Apples

Serves 4

Ingredients:

4	large	unpared apples
4	tablespoons	granulated or packed brown sugar
4	teaspoons	margarine or butter
½	teaspoon	ground cinnamon

Directions:

Heat oven to 375F. Core apples. Pare 1-inch strip of skin around middle of each apple, or pare upper half of each to prevent splitting. Place apples in ungreased baking dish. Place 1 teaspoon to 1 tablespoon sugar, 1 teaspoon margarine and ¼ teaspoon cinnamon in center of each apple. Sprinkle with cinnamon. Pour water into baking dish until ¼ inch deep. Bake 30 to 40 minutes, or until tender when pierced with fork. (Time will vary with size and variety of apple.) Spoon syrup in dish over apples several times during baking if desired. To microwave: Prepare apples as directed except omit water. Place each apple in 10 ounce custard cup or individual casseroles. Microwave uncovered on high 5 to 10 minutes, rotating cups ½ turn after 3 minutes, until apples are tender when pierced with fork.

Whole Wheat Chocolate Sheet Cake

Courtesy of The Wheat Foods Council
Serves 24

Ingredients:

2½	cups	whole wheat flour
1	cup	sugar
2	teaspoons	cinnamon
¼	cup	cocoa
1	cup	water
½	cup	vegetable oil
1½	teaspoons	baking soda
1	cup	buttermilk
2		eggs, beaten
1	teaspoon	vanilla

Optional icing:

¼	cup	cocoa
½	cup	butter or margarine
½	cup	low fat milk
3	cups	confectioner's sugar
½	cup	chopped nuts

Directions:

Heat oven to 350F. Mix flour, sugar, and cinnamon together in large bowl. Bring cocoa, water, and oil to boil. Pour over flour mixture and mix 1 minute, scraping bowl. Dissolve baking soda in buttermilk, adding to mixture in bowl, along with eggs and vanilla. Mix additional 2 minutes. Pour into greased and floured 10 x 5 x 1 inch jelly roll pan. Bake 20 minutes.
Icing: Bring cocoa, butter or margarine, and milk to a boil. Remove from heat and beat in sugar and nuts. Frost cake while still warm.

A gelatin dessert is always a welcome treat.

After-School Gelatin Snacks

Serves 6

Ingredients:

1	can	frozen grape juice concentrate, thawed
3		envelopes unflavored gelatin
1½	cups	(1 can) water

Directions:

Boil the water, add the juice concentrate and gelatin stirring until the gelatin dissolves. Remove from heat, pour into a lightly greased 9 x 13 pan and chill. Cut into squares when firm. Refrigerate in a covered container. This is good lunch box and traveling fare. It can go unrefrigerated for up to 4 hours under normal weather conditions.
Variations: Substitute frozen cranberry juice cocktail concentrate for grape juice, or a 12 ounce can of frozen apple or pear juice concentrate.

Mom's Best Gelatin Mold

Serves 4

Ingredients:

1		18-ounce jar or can of cherries
1		envelope gelatin
1	cup	cranberry juice
		sugar to taste

Directions:

To be served with cold chicken, turkey, or duck. Drain the cherries. Add their juice to the cold cranberry juice and sprinkle the gelatin over the liquid. Heat until almost simmering. Remove from heat, stir in the gelatin until it is thoroughly dissolved, and then add sugar, if needed. Pour into a 4-cup mold and cool. Pit the cherries, if necessary. When the liquid is about the consistency of egg whites, spoon in the cherries and chill until set. Serve garnished with watercress and cream cheese balls.

Cherry Gelatin

Serves 6

Ingredients:

3	ounces	flavored gelatin, any flavor
8	ounces	cream cheese
½	cup	nuts, if desired
8	ounces	cola, cold
1	cup	dark cherries, pitted, drained

Directions:
Dissolve flavored gelatin in boiling water. When cooled to room temperature, add cola, cream cheese, cherries, and nuts, if desired. Pour into 6-cup mold. Chill until set. Unmold to serve.

Cherry Waldorf Gelatin

Serves 8

Ingredients:

2	cups	boiling water
6	ounces	(1 package) cherry flavor gelatin
1	cup	cold water
¼	cup	lemon juice
1½	cups	chopped, cored apples
1	cup	chopped celery
1	cup	chopped walnuts or pecans

lettuce leaves
garnishes*

Directions:
In medium bowl, pour boiling water over gelatin. Stir until dissolved. Add cold water and lemon juice. Chill until partially set. Fold in apples, celery, and nuts. Pour into lightly oiled 6-cup mold or 9-inch square baking pan. Chill until set, 4 to 6 hours or overnight. Unmold on lettuce leaves and garnish as desired.
* Garnishes to include apple slices and/or celery leaves.

Rainbow Gelatin Dessert

Serves 20

Ingredients:

1	3 ounce box	strawberry flavored gelatin
1	3 ounce box	lime flavored gelatin
1	3 ounce box	orange flavored gelatin
1	3 ounce box	lemon flavored gelatin
4	envelopes	unflavored gelatin
4	cups	boiling water
2	cups	hot water
3		envelopes unflavored gelatin
1	can	sweetened condensed milk

Directions:
For flavored gelatin layers: Mix each of the four flavors of gelatin in individual bowls with 1 cup boiling water. Let cool.
For filling: Mix and dissolve in saucepan the hot water and unflavored gelatin. Add sweetened condensed milk and heat over low flame. Bring to a boil, stirring occasionally. Let cool. Place a 9 x 13 inch clear baking pan in the freezer, leveled evenly. Pour in first flavor of gelatin. Let set about 4 minutes, until flavored gelatin is lightly set. Pour ¾ cup filling over set flavored gelatin.

Mom was not always strict about between meal snacks.

Let set about 4 minutes. Repeat layers with other flavors of flavored gelatin and filling.
Note: Be sure flavored gelatin and filling layers are cool before adding next layer.

Mom's Favorite Strawberry Gelatin Dessert

Serves 8

Ingredients:

1	package	strawberry flavored gelatin
2	cups	boiling water
3		bananas, mashed
1	large can	crushed pineapple
30	ounces	frozen strawberries, drained
1	package	sour cream, large

Directions:
Mix flavored gelatin and 2 cups boiling water and let cool. Add mashed bananas, pineapple, and drained frozen strawberries. Put half the mixture into 13 x 9 x 2 inch pan and chill 30-45 minutes. Spread sour cream on top. Add remaining fruit and flavored gelatin mixture, chill, and cut into squares.

Mom's Best Bread Pudding

Serves 6

Ingredients:

1		egg
½	cup	sugar
2	cups	milk
1½	cups	bread cubes
1	teaspoon	cinnamon
½	teaspoon	cloves
½	teaspoon	allspice
¼	teaspoon	nutmeg
1	teaspoon	butter, melted
¼	teaspoon	salt
1½	cups	chocolate chips

Directions:

Beat egg until light. Add sugar and milk, then pour over torn up bread cubes. Add spices, butter, salt, and chocolate chips. Stir well. Pour into a baking dish. Set this in a pan of water and bake in a slow oven (300F) for 45 to 50 minutes, or until firm. Serve as is, with milk or cream on it or with any sauce. Also good cold.

Grandma's Home-Made Bread Pudding

Serves 6

Ingredients:

2	cups	milk
4	cups	dry bread, torn in pieces
¼	cup	melted butter
½	cup	sugar
2		eggs, slightly beaten
¼	teaspoon	salt
½	cup	seedless raisins
1	teaspoon	cinnamon (optional)

strawberries and whipped cream

Directions:

Butter a 1½ quart casserole dish and set aside. Heat milk to scalding and pour over bread. Lightly mix, then allow to cool. Add remaining ingredients, stir well, and pour into casserole dish.
Bake at 350F for 40 to 50 minutes, or until knife inserted into center comes out clean. Serve warm. Even better when topped with fresh or frozen strawberries and whipped cream.

Steamed Bread Pudding

Serves 6

Ingredients:

1	cup	brown sugar
2	cups	milk
½	cup	seedless raisins
1	teaspoon	vanilla extract
5		thin slices white bread
½	teaspoon	ground cinnamon
¼	teaspoon	salt
¼	cup	(½ stick) butter, softened
3		eggs

Directions:

In the top of an oiled double boiler, mix the brown sugar and raisins. Remove crusts from bread, butter the slices on one side, and then cut them into ½ inch cubes. You should have about 2 cups. Place the cubes on top of the brown sugar mixture. In a medium bowl, beat the eggs lightly. Then add the remaining ingredients, but just blend, don't over-mix. Pour the egg mixture over the bread cubes, but do not stir in. Cook, covered, over simmering water, for about 1 hour and 20 minutes. A knife inserted in the center should come out fairly clean. (Pudding will continue cooking after taken out of pan, so don't worry if it is still a bit shaky at the end of the cooking time.) Immediately loosen the edges of the pudding with a rubber spatula and invert onto a 12 inch round platter with a lip. Arrange any stray raisins decoratively around the edge of the platter. Serve warm.

Mom's Dessert Waldorf

Serves 4

Ingredients:

2	medium	apples, coarsely chopped (about 2 cups)
1	medium	stalk celery, chopped (about ½ cup)
½	cup	mayonnaise or salad dressing
½	cup	coarsely chopped nuts
1	can	(8 ounces) pineapple chunks, drained
½	cup	miniature marshmallows
½	cup	chopped dates

Directions:

Toss all ingredients. Serve on salad greens if desired.

Grandma's Apple Strudel

Serves 6

Ingredients:

6	cups	apples, tart, sliced
¾	cup	raisins
1	tablespoon	lemon rind, grated
¾	cup	sugar
2	teaspoons	cinnamon
¾	cup	almonds, ground
8	ounces	phyllo leaves, ½ box, thawed
1¾	cups	butter (not margarine), melted
1	cup	bread crumbs, finely crushed

Directions:

Mix apples with raisins, lemon rind, sugar, cinnamon, and almonds. Set aside. Place 1 phyllo leaf on a kitchen towel and brush with melted butter. Place a second leaf on top and brush with butter again. Repeat until 5 leaves have been used, using about ½ cup of butter. Cook and stir bread crumbs with ¼ cup of butter until lightly browned. Sprinkle ¾ cup crumbs on the layered phyllo leaves. Mound ½ of the filling in a 3 inch strip along the narrow end of the phyllo, leaving a 2 inch border. Lift towel, using it to roll leaves over apples, jelly roll fashion. Brush top of the strudel with butter and sprinkle with 2 tablespoon crumbs. Repeat the entire procedure for the second strudel. Bake the strudels at 400F for 20 to 25 minutes, until browned. Makes 2 strudels, 6 to 8 servings each.
Note: Frozen phyllo leaves for strudel can be found at most supermarkets in the frozen foods section.

Favorite Apple Dumplings

Serves 6

Ingredients:

2	cups	flour
2	teaspoons	baking powder
1	teaspoon	salt
6	tablespoons	shortening
½	cup	cold milk
6		medium apples, pared and cored
½	cup	sugar
2	teaspoons	cinnamon

Directions:

Sift flour, baking powder, and salt together. Cut in shortening, add milk, and mix to a smooth dough. Turn onto floured surface and divide into 6 portions. Roll each portion large enough to cover 1 apple. Place an apple on each piece of pastry. Mix sugar and

cinnamon together. Spoon some of this mixture into each core cavity. Moisten edges of pastry and bring up over the apple. Seal edges. Place on greased baking sheet or in shallow pan. Bake at 350F , or until apples are tender and pastry is lightly browned. Remove from baking sheet. Serve warm with milk or cream.

Grandma's Basic Old-Fashioned Fruit Cobbler

Serves 4

Ingredients:

¾		stick butter
¾	cup	flour
¾	cup	milk
1	cup	sugar
2	teaspoons	baking powder
2	cups	sweetened fruit

Directions:

Melt butter in deep casserole dish. Mix sugar, flour, baking powder, and milk together. Pour over melted butter. Don't stir. On top, pour 2 cups sweetened fruit. Bake for 45 minutes to 1 hour at 325F.

Christmas Figgy Pudding

Serves 6

Ingredients:

2	½ cups	soft bread crumbs
½	cup	milk
3		eggs
½	cup	finely chopped butter
1	cup	brown or light brown sugar
	1	cup	chopped figs
½	teaspoon	salt

Directions:

Soak bread crumbs in milk. Chop the butter into very small pieces. Chop or cut figs into small pieces. Mix all ingredients together and put into a buttered mold with cover (or can be cooked in top pot of double boiler). Steam for 4 hours.
Serve with whipped cream, or vanilla ice cream.
Dates may be substituted for figs.

Apple Raisin Bread Pudding

Courtesy of The American Egg Board
Serves 8

Ingredients:

2	tablespoons	butter
2	cups	chopped, cored cooking apples (about 2 medium)
3	cups	day-old white bread cubes (about 3 slices)
½	cup	raisins
4		eggs
2	cups	milk
½	cup	firmly-packed brown sugar
1	teaspoon	vanilla
¾	teaspoon	pumpkin pie spice

whipped cream or ice cream, optional
apple wedges, optional

Directions:

In small saucepan over medium heat, melt butter. Stir in chopped apples. Cover and cook over medium heat, stirring occasionally, until slightly soft, about 5 to 7 minutes. In shallow 1½ quart casserole, lightly toss together apples, bread cubes, and raisins. Beat together eggs, milk, sugar, vanilla, and spice until sugar is dissolved. Pour over apple mixture. Cover and refrigerate several hours or overnight. Bake in preheated, 350F oven until knife inserted near center comes out clean, 45 to 55 minutes. Serve hot, warm, or chilled, garnished with whipped cream and/or apple wedges if desired.

Mom's Basic Double Crust Pie

Ingredients:

1½	cups	flour
½	teaspoon	salt
½	cup	shortening
4	tablespoons	cold water

Directions:

Sift the flour with salt. Blend in the shortening, using a fork or pastry knife. When it is the consistency of cornmeal, add the cold water. Do not use more water, because too much water makes a tough crust. Work lightly together into a ball. Turn onto a floured pastry board. Divide into 2 portions. Roll the pastry into a ¼ inch thick circle. Fit the pastry neatly over the pie plate, leaving about 1 inch projecting over the rim of the pan. Be sure there are no cracks in the pastry of the bottom crust. If there are any cracks, seal them by pressing the edges together with your finger. Use any desired filling. Moisten the edges of the pastry with cold water. Fit the top crust over the pie. Press the edges together firmly. Trim the overhanging pastry even with the edge of the pan. Mark the rim with a fork or a pastry marker. Bake the pie at 450F for 10 minutes. Reduce heat and bake at 325F according to the recipe instructions. Before putting the pie into the oven cut slits in the top crust to allow the steam to escape. A larger amount of dough may be made by increasing the ingredients, keeping their proper proportions. The pastry dough may be kept

The promise of Apple Raisin Bread Pudding always kept people lingering at the table when dinner was finished.

in a refrigerator indefinitely. Wrap in a towel or waxed paper and use as needed. If the pastry dough is chilled before using, it will make a lighter crust. Makes one 9-inch pie.

Mom's Basic Single Crust Pie

Ingredients:

1	cup	sifted flour
1	teaspoon	baking powder
1	tablespoon	sugar
¼	teaspoon	salt
½	cup	butter or margarine
1	tablespoon	cold water

Directions:
Mix pastry as directed for Mom's Basic Mom's Basic Double Crust Pie (see above). Roll into a single circle of pastry. Place the pastry in the bottom of a pie pan. Then double any overhanging dough onto the edge of the pie pan and pinch this with your fingers and thumbs all around the edge to make a fancy border. Prick all over bottom and around the sides to prevent pastry from puffing up while baking. Bake at 425F. Place the shell as close to the center of the oven as possible and bake until a creamy brown, about 12 minutes. Cool before filling. This recipe can be doubled or tripled and the extra baked crusts wrapped securely in plastic wrap, frozen and then stacked in a plastic bag for future use. Thaw completely before using. Makes one 9-inch single crust pie.

Mom's Berry Pie

Serves 6

Ingredients:

1	Mom's Basic Double Crust recipe	
4	cups	berries
1	cup	sugar
1	tablespoon	flour

Directions:
This recipe will do for any berry, such as blueberry, raspberry, loganberry, or blackberry. Stir berries, sugar, and flour together. Prepare Mom's Basic Double Crust Pie recipes. Pour fruit into bottom crust and cover with top crust or cut the top crust into strips which are then laid over the fruit to form an open design. Bake at 450F for 10 minutes. Reduce heat to 325F and bake for 20 minutes longer. Place on window ledge to cool.

Fresh out of the oven is always best.

Mom's Blueberry Cream Pie

Serves 6

Ingredients:

1	Mom's Basic Single Crust recipe	
1	package	blueberries
1	cup	sugar
1	cup	water
2	tablespoons	cornstarch
¼	cup	cold water
1	cup	whipping cream

Directions:
To prepare the blueberries, remove stems and wash thoroughly, then place 1 cup of them in a pot with the sugar and water. Allow these to boil for 5 minutes (a slow boil). Strain through wire sieve, crushing the berries with a spoon. When all the juice is squeezed from the berries, throw away the pulp and return the juice to the pot. Dissolve the cornstarch in the cold water and add to the juice. Stir constantly while adding, until the mixture again comes to a boil. Then simmer about 30 minutes very slowly until it is a thick, heavy syrup. When the syrup is thickened, pour the boiling syrup over the fresh blueberries. Stir and put them away to thoroughly chill. Prepare Mom's Basic Single Crust recipe. Whip cream and fill the pastry shell with the whipped cream, spreading it level. On top of the whipped cream place the berries and heavy syrup.

Mom's Cherry Pie

Serves 6

Ingredients:

1		Mom's Basic Double Crust recipe
3	cups	pitted pie cherries
1	cup	sugar
1	tablespoon	flour

Directions:

Mix the pie cherries with sugar and flour. Prepare one of Mom's Basic Double Crust Pie recipes. Pour filling into pan. Dot with 2 tablespoons butter. Add top crust. Bake at 450F for 10 minutes, then reduce heat to 325F and bake 25 minutes. Place on window ledge to cool.

Mom's Special Pineapple-Cranberry Pie

Serves 6

Ingredients:

1		Mom's Basic Double Crust recipe
2	cups	cranberries
1	cup	drained, crushed pineapple
1	cup	sugar

Directions:

Put the cranberries through the food chopper. Add the drained, crushed pineapple and sugar. Prepare Mom's Basic Double Crust recipe. Pour fruit into bottom crust and cut the top crust into strips. Then lay them over the fruit to form an open lattice design. Bake 10 minutes at 400F. Finish baking at 350F for 20 minutes. Place on window ledge to cool.

Mom's Basic Apple Pie

Serves 6

Ingredients:

1		Mom's Basic Double Crust recipe
4	cups	sliced apples (1 quart)
1	cup	sugar (less if desired)
1	teaspoon	sifted flour
½	teaspoon	cinnamon or nutmeg
3	tablespoons	water

Directions:

Peel, core, and thinly slice apples. Mix the sugar and flour together thoroughly and put into the bowl with the apples. Stir the mixture and add the water. Stir again once or twice. Make pastry as directed in Mom's Basic Double Crust Pie recipes. Pour apple mixture into the pie crust. Be sure there are no cracks in the pastry of the bottom crust. If there are any cracks, seal them by pressing the edges together with your finger. When the fruit is in the pie, distribute it evenly and put the top crust on by rolling it onto the rolling pin and unrolling it on top of the fruit. Place the pie as near the center of the oven as possible and bake at 450F for 15 minutes. Then reduce to 325F for a further 25 or 30 minutes. Place on window ledge to cool.

Mom's Deep Dish Apple Pie

Serves 6

Ingredients:

1		Mom's Basic Double Crust recipe
2	pounds	cooking apples (should have sufficient apples when sliced to slightly mound in the dish)
1	cup	sugar
½	teaspoon	cinnamon, cloves or grated lemon rind, as preferred
1	tablespoon	flour
water		

Directions:

Wash fruit. If using apples, remove cores and thinly slice. Make pastry as directed in Mom's Basic Double Crust Pie recipes except use a deep dish pie pan instead of a regular size pan. Place in the center of a deep pie pan a small inverted cup. (This inverted cup, or other small utensil, serves two purposes. It acts as a bridge to hold up the pastry in the center of the pie, and it also draws up the juices in a way that will astonish those who do not know this old country tip.) Place the fruit in the pie dish, enough to slightly mound the dish. Mix together the sugar and tablespoon flour and pour it into the dish with the fruit (the flour gives a slight body to the juice) and stir it down into the fruit as much as possible. Next wash down the rest of the sugar from the top by pouring in slowly sufficient water to fill the dish one quarter full. Preheat oven to 425F and place the pie as near the center of the oven as possible. Bake for 10 minutes, then reduce the heat of the oven to 325F and allow to bake for 40 minutes in all. Place on window ledge to cool.

Mom's Baked Apple Dessert

Serves 6

Ingredients:

4		apples
1¼	cups	sugar
1	teaspoon	cinnamon
1	teaspoon	nutmeg (optional)
1	cup	water

Directions:

Core, but do not peel the apples. Place in a baking pan. Into the center of each apple, pour 3 level tablespoons of sugar. This fills the center of the apple to overflowing. On top of the sugar add ¼ teaspoon cinnamon. Then pour water into the pan to a depth of ¾ inch. Allow the pan of apples to stand undisturbed for a few moments. Then push a wire skewer down through sugar, which causes sugar and cinnamon to run into the center of the apple. Next add two more level tablespoons of sugar to each apple, pouring the sugar over the center of the apple. (This makes a total of five level tablespoons of sugar to each apple.)

Place the pan near the center of the oven and bake at 400F until apples crack open. Then carefully turn the apples over with a large spoon. Continue baking until thoroughly soft. Baste occasionally while baking. A few drops of lemon can be added with the sugar and cinnamon if desired. Place on window ledge to cool.

Grandma's Favorite Old-Fashioned Apple Betty

Serves 6

Directions:

3	cups	sliced apples
1	cup	soft white bread, broken into small pieces
¼	cup	butter or margarine
¾	cup	sugar
1	teaspoon	nutmeg
½	cup	water
¼	teaspoon	salt

Directions:

Place in buttered pudding dish (or deep pie pan) one layer of sliced apples and a layer of broken white bread (or cut into small fingers). Sprinkle well with sugar and just a pinch of nutmeg, then put little dabs of butter all over the top. Repeat, in the same order, one layer on top of another, until the dish is full. Add the salt to the water and pour into dish. Bake at 350F for 45 to 50 minutes. Place on window ledge to cool. Bread should be nicely browned on top.

Mom's Cherry Cream Pie

Serves 6

Ingredients:

1	can	sweet black cherries (or pie cherries)
½	cup	sugar
½	cup	cold water
1½	tablespoons	cornstarch

Directions:

Strain juice from cherries into small pot and add the sugar. Dissolve the cornstarch in the cold water, and add this to the juice and sugar. Bring this mixture to a boil and allow to simmer very slowly for half an hour. While the liquid is simmering, split the cherries in half and remove the stones, putting the cherries in a bowl. Then pour the heavy syrup from the pot over the cherries and chill.

Grandma's Chocolate Almond Cream Pie Filling

Serves 6

Ingredients:

1	cup	milk
2	ounces	unsweetened chocolate (2 squares)
2		eggs
¼	cup	sugar
1	tablespoon	powdered gelatin
2	tablespoons	cold water
¼	teaspoon	cinnamon
¾	teaspoon	vanilla
¼	teaspoon	salt
½	cup	whipping cream
½	cup	almonds
1	tablespoon	olive oil

Directions:

Soak the gelatin in the cold water. Cook the almonds in boiling water for a few minutes and then remove skins. Cut in pieces and brown slightly by placing in pan with olive oil.

Place pan over medium low heat and stir the almonds until slightly browned. Remove from oil and allow to cool. Melt chocolate. Separate the eggs. Put sugar and egg yolks into the top of double boiler and stir to thoroughly break up the yolks.

Add the milk and melted chocolate and cinnamon and cook in double boiler, gently stirring until the mixture begins to thicken. Then remove pot from stove. Add the soaked gelatin and stir until it is dissolved. When cool, add the stiffly beaten whites of eggs, vanilla, and salt and fold together by passing the spoon through the egg white, down and along under the mixture, then up and over the egg white again.

When thoroughly blended, beat the whipping cream until stiff. Fold in.

Finally, add the browned almonds. Gently stir them into the mixture, and place the whole mixture in a mold. Put it in the refrigerator to chill. When set, serve with whipped cream.

Mom's Special Date Pie

Serves 6

Ingredients:

1		Mom's Basic Single Crust recipe
2		eggs
¾	cup	sugar
2	tablespoons	flour
¼	teaspoon	cloves
¼	teaspoon	nutmeg
1	teaspoon	cinnamon
1	cup	cream
1	cup	pitted dates
coconut to taste		

Directions:

Prepare Single Crust recipe. Separate the eggs. Beat the yolks, add sugar and beat. Add flour mixed with cloves, nutmeg and cinnamon. Add to the egg and sugar mixture. Blend. Add cream and finely cut up dates. Beat the egg whites until stiff. Add to the mixture. Put the filling in the pastry and sprinkle the top with coconut. Bake for 10 minutes at 450F. Reduce heat and bake 30 minutes at 325F. Place on window ledge to cool.

Fresh Cherry Pie from Scratch

Serves 6

Ingredients:

1	pound	cherries
1¼	cup	water
1	cup	sugar
1½	tablespoons	cornstarch
1		Mom's Basic Double Crust recipe
1	cup	whipping cream

Directions:

Wash and cook the cherries in 1 cup of water and sugar for 10 minutes. Strain the juice from the cherries. Dissolve the cornstarch in ¼ cup of cold water and pour into juice. Return juice to heat and stir constantly until it boils. Slowly simmer for 30 minutes. In the meantime split cherries into halves and remove stones. Then pour the heavy syrup over the pitted cherries, stir, place in refrigerator and chill, or combine the pie at the time you want to serve it.
Prepare Mom's Basic Single Crust recipe. Whip the cream until stiff and fill the pastry shell. Place the cold cherries and heavy syrup over the whipped cream. Serve.

Peach Cobbler

Courtesy of The Wheat Foods Council
  Serves 6-8

Ingredients:
Fruit:

2	24 ounce cans	juice-packed, sliced peaches, drained
	or	
2¼	pounds	fresh peaches, peeled and sliced
¼	cup	granulated sugar
1	teaspoon	cinnamon
1	tablespoon	cornstarch (optional)

Cobbler topping mixture:

1	cup	all-purpose flour (may be all or part whole wheat)
1	tablespoon	granulated sugar
½	cup	1 percent milk
1	teaspoon	baking powder
1	pinch	salt
3	tablespoons	margarine or butter

Directions:

Fruit: Place in lightly oiled 8 x 8 inch baking dish. Mix sugar, cinnamon, and cornstarch. Sprinkle over fruit.
Preheat oven to 425F. Prepare baking dish with fruit. Combine flour, sugar, baking powder, and salt. Cut in margarine or butter. Stir in milk with fork until soft dough forms. Drop six to eight spoonfuls on top of peaches. (If desired, sprinkle a mixture of cinnamon and sugar on top.) Bake for 25-30 minutes, until topping is brown and bubbling around the edge. Place on window ledge to cool. Cool 10 minutes before serving.

Peach Cobbler is a welcome treat.

Mom's Fancy Lemon Chiffon Pie

Serves 6

Ingredients:

1		Mom's Basic Double Crust recipe
2	tablespoons	butter or margarine
1	cup	sugar
2		eggs
3	tablespoons	flour
1	cup	milk

juice and grated rind of 1 lemon

Directions:

Mix the butter with sugar. Separate the eggs and beat the yolks well, then add to sugar and butter. Add the flour and beat. Add the milk and beat well. Add the lemon juice and grated rind and mix. Beat the egg whites until stiff and fold in. Prepare Single Crust recipe. Pour filling into the pie shell. Bake 10 minutes at 450F. Then reduce heat to 325F and bake for 20 minutes. Place on ledge to cool.

Mom knows that taking pies from the oven is a spectator sport.

Mom's Favorite Lemon Meringue Pie

Ingredients:

1		Mom's Basic Single Crust recipe
1	cup	sugar
1	cup	boiling water
2		lemons, juice from
3	tablespoons	butter or margarine
3	tablespoons	flour
3		eggs
6	tablespoons	sugar

Directions:

Put 1 cup sugar into the top of a double boiler. Add the boiling water and the lemon juice. Blend butter with flour. Combine with the lemon mixture and cook in the double boiler until slightly thickened. Stir constantly. Separate the eggs. Add the well beaten yolks and cook 10 minutes. Stir occasionally. Cool until cold. The pie should not be put together until a few minutes before it is eaten. Prepare Mom's Basic Single Crust recipe and cool. Pour filling into baked pie shell. Make the meringue by beating the egg whites until stiff. Add the 6 tablespoons sugar. Pile the meringue on the pie. Bake at 500F for 3 minutes or less. Watch it closely and remove when a delicate brown on top. Place on window ledge to cool.

Mom's Legendary Autumn Afternoon, Home From School Pumpkin Pie

Serves 6

Ingredients:

1		Mom's Basic Double Crust recipe
2	cups	cooked pumpkin
1	cup	brown sugar
¾	teaspoon	ginger
¾	teaspoon	cinnamon
1	teaspoon	salt
2		eggs
1½	cups	milk

Directions:

Mix pumpkin, brown sugar, ginger, cinnamon, and salt together. Beat eggs slightly and add milk, stirring together. Add to pumpkin mixture and stir well. Prepare Single Crust recipe.
Pour pumpkin filling into unbaked pie shell. Bake at 450F for 15 minutes and then reduce to 350F for 1 hour or until custard is set. Test custard by inserting a knife just off center. If the knife pulls out clean, the pie is done. Place on the window ledge to cool.

Grandma's Pumpkin Pie

Serves 6

Ingredients:

1		Mom's Basic Double Crust recipe
4	tablespoons	flour
2	tablespoons	cinnamon
1	tablespoon	mace
1	level teaspoon	cloves
2	cups	brown sugar
4	cups	mashed pumpkin
4		eggs
½	cup	cream
½	cup	melted butter or margarine
½	cup	molasses

Directions:

Put 3 inches of water in the bottom of a large pot. Put another smaller pot upside down into the larger pot. Put over high heat. While the water is heating, peel, remove seeds and cut up a medium pumpkin. Lay pieces on top of small pot. If you are using sweet potatoes, wash and drop in whole. Steam until tender. Peel the sweet potatoes after steaming.

Mix the flour, cinnamon, mace, and cloves with brown sugar. Add to the pumpkin. Separate the eggs and beat in the yolks. Add the cream, melted butter and molasses. Fold in the beaten egg whites. Prepare Mom's Single Crust recipe in a deep dish pie pan. (This recipe will make 2 small pies or 1 very large pie.) Put into the oven at 450F for 10 minutes. Then reduce the heat to 325F for 20 minutes. Bake until the custard is set. Place on window ledge to cool. Whipped cream may be served on top.

Raisin Pie Filling

Serves 6

Ingredients:

1		Mom's Basic Double Crust Pie
1½	cups	seeded raisins
½	cup	sugar
2	tablespoons	flour
2	tablespoons	lemon juice
		grated rind of 1 lemon
1	cup	boiling water

Directions:

In a bowl place the raisins, sugar, and flour. Mix. Add the lemon juice, grated rind, and boiling water. Stir and chill. Prepare Mom's Basic Double Crust Pie and pour the filling into the bottom crust. Cover with top crust and bake 30 minutes at 450F. Place on window ledge to cool.

Grandma's Special Mince Meat

This is a quantity recipe to be made and kept for use when required in the making of Mince Meat Pies.

Ingredients:

3	cups	butter or margarine (1½ pounds)
3	pounds	apples
3	pounds	seeded raisins
1	pound	currants
1	pound	seedless raisins
2	pounds	citron
2	pounds	dates and/or figs
½	cup	candied orange peel
½	cup	candied lemon peel
½	cup	lemon juice
½	cup	orange juice
2	pounds	sugar (4 cups)
2	cups	cider
1	teaspoon	powdered cloves
1	teaspoon	allspice
1	teaspoon	cinnamon
2	teaspoons	grated nutmeg
1	teaspoon	almond extract
2	cups	brandy
1	cup	sherry
2	tablespoons	salt

Directions:

Put all the ingredients, except the seedless raisins and liquids, through a meat grinder. If you do not have a grinder then chop the ingredients very fine (but a grinder is best). Place all ingredients, except the brandy and sherry, into a large pot and allow to slowly cook for 2 ½ to 3 hours. Stir every now and then to keep from sticking and burning. Remove from stove and add the brandy and sherry. Keep in crock or tightly capped in mason jars. It is better if allowed to stand for about a week before using. To make a Mince Meat Pie, use Mom's Basic Double Crust Pie recipe with the Mince Meat for the filling.

Pineapple Cream Pie

Serves 6

Ingredients:

1		Mom's Basic Single Crust recipe
6	slices	canned pineapple
½	cup	sugar
1	cup	pineapple juice
1	cup	whipping cream

Directions:
Strain all the juice from the pineapple. There should be a little more than 1 cup of juice but if not, use as near a cupful as possible, reserving 2 tablespoons juice. Put the cup of juice and sugar into a saucepan or bright clean skillet. Then add the slices of pineapple that have been cut into squares and bring to a boil.
Allow it to boil rapidly for about 9 or 10 minutes, until the juice begins to show slight signs of threading when it drops from a spoon. (The drip from a spoon should not drip like water, but begin to show signs of dripping with a thread.) Another sign to watch for is that the juice will begin to turn to a very light golden brown. Then remove the pineapple from stove and pour it into a china or earthenware bowl. Do not use a glass bowl because the pineapple is very hot and might crack it. Cool, then chill in refrigerator. If the syrup is too thick when cool, it can be easily thinned by adding a little of the reserved pineapple juice.
Prepare Mom's Basic Single Crust recipe. At serving time, fill the pastry shell with whipped cream, then carefully spread the pineapple in the heavy candied syrup over the whipped cream.

Raspberry Cream Pie

Serves 6

Ingredients:
1		Mom's Basic Single Crust recipe
1	pound	raspberries
½	cup	sugar
¾	cup	cold water
1½	tablespoons	cornstarch
1	cup	whipping cream

Directions:
Select half a cup of the poorer berries, wash thoroughly, and place in a pot with the sugar and ½ cup cold water. Allow these to boil for 15 minutes at a slow boil, then strain through wire sieve, crushing the berries with a spoon.
When all the juice is squeezed from the berries throw away the pulp and return the juice to the pot. Dissolve the cornstarch in ¼ cup water and add. Stir constantly while adding until the mixture again comes to a boil, then simmer very slowly until it becomes a thick, heavy syrup. While the syrup is simmering, wash the rest of the raspberries. When the raspberry syrup has simmered down to a heavy syrup, cool but do not chill. Pour the syrup over the raspberries and put into the refrigerator to chill.
Prepare Mom's Basic Single Crust recipe. To serve, whip the cream and fill the pastry shell with it, spreading level. Then place the cold raspberries and heavy syrup on top of the whipped cream.

Home-Style Rhubarb Pie

Serves 6

Ingredients:
1		Mom's Basic Double Crust recipe
3	heaping cups	cut rhubarb
1¼	cups	sugar
3	tablespoons	flour
2	tablespoons	butter or margarine

Directions:
Prepare Mom's Basic Double Crust recipe. Mix rhubarb, sugar, and flour together and pour fruit into bottom crust. Dot with butter. Cut the top crust into strips and then lay them over the fruit to form an open lattice design. Press edges together and trim. Bake in oven at 400F for 10 minutes and then reduce to 375F for 20 minutes. Place on window ledge to cool.

Strawberry Cream Pie

Serves 6

Ingredients:
1		Mom's Basic Single Crust recipe
4	cups	strawberries (1 quart)
1	cup	sugar
1¼	cup	cold water
3	tablespoons	cornstarch
1	cup	whipping cream

Directions:
Select one cup of the poorer berries, removing stems and washing thoroughly. Place in a pot with the sugar and one cup water. Bring to a boil and slowly boil 15 to 20 minutes. Strain through wire sieve, crushing the berries with a spoon. When all the juice is squeezed from the berries, throw away the pulp and return the juice to the pot. Dissolve the cornstarch in ¼ cup water and add. Stir constantly while adding until the mixture again comes to a boil. Simmer very slowly until it becomes a thick, heavy syrup.
While the syrup is cooking, prepare the rest of the strawberries by washing, removing stems, and removing the little white hard center from the strawberries. This can easily be done with a small, pointed knife. When the strawberries are cleaned and prepared, cut them into halves, or quarters, according to the size of the strawberries. Then pour the boiling syrup over them and put into refrigerator to chill.
Prepare Mom's Basic Single Crust recipe. To serve, whip the cream and fill the pastry shell with it, spreading level. Then place the cold strawberries and heavy syrup on top of the whipped cream.

Mom's Famous Orange Pie

Serves 6

Ingredients:

1		Mom's Basic Single Crust recipe
1	cup	orange juice
3	tablespoons	lemon juice
1	cup	sugar
¼	cup	flour
½	teaspoon	salt
1		orange rind
3		egg yolks
3	tablespoons	butter or margarine

Meringue Ingredients:

3		egg whites
6	tablespoons	sugar
1	teaspoon	vanilla

Meringue Directions:

Add the lemon juice to the orange juice. Mix ½ cup sugar with the flour and salt. Grate in the rind of the orange. Add the liquid to the dry ingredients. Cook over hot water for 10 minutes, stirring occasionally. Separate the eggs and beat the egg yolks. Beat in ½ cup sugar. Remove the orange mixture from the heat. Beat in the eggs. Add butter. Cook for 3 minutes, beating constantly. Place on window ledge to cool.
Prepare Mom's Basic Single Crust recipe. At serving time place the orange filling in the pie shell. Whip the egg whites until stiff. Add 6 tablespoons sugar and vanilla.

Fresh from the oven!

Pile this on the pie. Set in a 500F oven. Brown the top delicately. This should take 3 minutes or less. Watch the pie carefully or it will burn. Place on window ledge to cool.

Mom's Festive Mint Cookies

Serves about 24 to 36

Ingredients:

10	ounces	mint chocolate wafers
¾	cup	butter, softened
½	cup	sugar
1		egg
¼	teaspoon	salt
1½	cups	unsifted flour
¾	cup	finely chopped walnuts

Directions:

Melt 5 ounces of the mint wafers in a double boiler, stirring constantly, or microwave on medium for about 3 minutes. Set aside. Cream butter with sugar, egg, and salt. Mix in melted chocolate. Gradually add flour. Chill dough for at least 1 hour. Shape dough into balls, using 1 level tablespoon for each cookie. Roll balls in nuts. Place on greased baking sheets. Flatten slightly with the palm of hand. Bake at 350F for only 8 minutes. Remove from oven and place mint wafer on top of each cookie, pressing slightly. Continue baking 3 to 5 minutes longer, or until cookie is firm.

Applesauce Cookies

Serves about 24

Ingredients:

1	cup	unsweetened applesauce
1	cup	sugar
½	cup	butter or lard
1		egg
2	cups	flour
1	cup	raisins, chopped
1	cup	nut meats
1	teaspoon	baking powder
1	teaspoon	baking soda
1	teaspoon	cinnamon
1	teaspoon	cloves
¼	teaspoon	salt

Directions:

Combine ingredients. Then drop by teaspoonfuls onto greased cookie sheets. Bake in 375F oven until done. Place on window ledge to cool.

Favorite Chocolate Chip Cookies

Serves 72

Ingredients:

¾	cup	margarine, softened
¾	cup	shortening
1½	cups	brown sugar, light, packed
¾	cup	sugar
3		eggs
3	tablespoons	corn syrup, light
3	tablespoons	water
3	teaspoons	vanilla
3¾	cups	flour, unsifted
1½	teaspoons	baking soda
¾	teaspoon	salt
3	cups	chocolate chips, semisweet

Directions:

Cream margarine, shortening, sugars, eggs, corn syrup, water, and vanilla. Beat well. Combine flour, baking soda, and salt. Add to creamed mixture. Beat well. Stir in chips. Drop by rounded teaspoonfuls. Bake at 350F for 15 minutes. Allow to cool on cookie sheet for 1 minute. Place on window ledge to cool.

One of the great joys of life: Cookies and milk.

Basic Peanut Butter Cookies

Serves 6

Ingredients:

14	ounces	sweetened condensed milk (not evaporated milk)
¾-1	cup	peanut butter
1		egg
1	teaspoon	vanilla extract
2	cups	biscuit baking mix
		granulated sugar

Directions:

Preheat your oven to 350F. In large mixer bowl, beat sweetened condensed milk, peanut butter, egg, and vanilla extract until smooth. Add biscuit mix and mix well. Chill at least 1 hour. Shape into 1-inch balls. Roll in sugar. Place 2 inches apart on ungreased baking sheets. Flatten with fork. Bake 6 to 8 minutes, or until lightly browned. (Do not overbake). Place on a window ledge to cool. Store it tightly covered at room temperature.

Mom's Coconut Cookies

Serves 48

Ingredients:

¼	cup	shortening
¾	cup	sugar
¼	cup	water
1	teaspoon	vanilla
1	teaspoon	baking powder
½	teaspoon	salt
¼	cup	walnuts
½	cup	finely shredded coconut

Directions:

Beat shortening until soft. Add sugar and cream until fluffy. Add water and mix. Add the rest of the ingredients in order, mixing well after each addition. Finish with the nuts and the coconut. Form into rolls, wrap in waxed paper and chill for several hours in the refrigerator. Slice into rounds ¼ inch thick. Bake on an ungreased cookie sheet for 10 minutes at 375F. Place on window ledge to cool.

Favorite Sugar Cookies

Serves 3

Ingredients:

¼	cup	shortening
¼	cup	margarine
2	cups	all-purpose flour
¾	cup	sugar
1		egg
1	tablespoon	milk
1	teaspoon	baking powder
1	teaspoon	vanilla extract

Directions:

In a large bowl, beat the shortening and margarine with an electric mixer at medium to high speed for about 30 seconds, or until softened. Add about half of the flour and all of the remaining ingredients and beat until thoroughly combined, scraping the sides of the bowl occasionally. Beat or stir in the remaining flour. Divide the dough in half. Cover and chill for 1 to 2 hours, or until easy to handle. Roll each portion of the dough to ¼ inch thickness on a lightly floured surface. Cut into the desired shapes. Place 1 inch apart on an ungreased cookie sheet. If desired, sprinkle with candies or colored sugar before baking. Bake in a 375F oven for 7 to 9 minutes, or until the edges are firm and the bottoms are very lightly browned. Remove the cookies and cool on a rack. Makes 3 to 4 dozen cookies. Chocolate sugar cookies: Stir 1 tablespoon of unsweetened cocoa powder into one half of the recipe. Bake as directed.

Mom's Brown Sugar Cookies

Serves 15

Ingredients:

¼	cup	butter or butter substitute
½	cup	brown sugar
2		eggs
½	cup	milk
1	cup	flour
1	teaspoon	baking powder
½	teaspoon	salt
¾	cup	chopped nuts

Directions:

Cream butter. Add sugar. Add eggs, yolks and whites beaten separately, and milk. Sift flour, measure, and sift again with baking powder and salt. Add to first mixture. Add nuts. Mix thoroughly. Drop by teaspoonfuls onto well-oiled baking sheet. Bake in moderate oven (400F) for about 15 minutes. Nuts or raisins may be pressed into each cookie before baking.

Chocolate Meringue Cookies

Serves 20

Ingredients:

2		egg whites
¼	teaspoon	cream of tartar
¾	cup	sugar
1	package	6 ounces chocolate chips

Directions:

Preheat your oven to 350F. Beat 2 egg whites. Add ¼ teaspoon cream of tartar, ¾ cup sugar and beat stiff. Fold in 6 ounce package of chocolate chips. Drop batter by the teaspoonful onto greased cookie sheet. Turn off oven, put in cookies and leave in oven overnight. Do not open oven door until morning.

The Gingerbread Man

Serves 24

Ingredients:

1	cup	butter or margarine
½	cup	brown sugar
½	cup	corn syrup and/or molasses
4	cups	flour
1½	teaspoons	cinnamon
1	teaspoon	ginger
½	teaspoon	ground cloves
¾	teaspoon	baking soda
1		egg, lightly beaten
1½	teaspoons	vanilla extract

Directions:

In a saucepan combine butter, brown sugar, and corn syrup or molasses. Cook and stir over medium heat until sugar dissolves. Pour into large mixing bowl. Cool 5 minutes. Sift together flour, cinnamon, ginger, cloves and baking soda. Add egg and vanilla to butter mixture. Mix well. Add flour mixture and beat until well mixed. Divide dough in half, cover and chill 2 hours or overnight. For each man (or person), shape dough into one 1 inch ball, one ¾ inch ball, six ½ inch balls and one ¼ inch ball. On ungreased cookie sheet flatten the 1 inch ball to ½ inch thickness for body. Attach the ¾ inch ball for head and flatten to ½ inch thickness. Attach the ½ inch balls for arms, legs and ears. Attach the ¼ inch ball for nose. Bake at 350F for 8 to 10 minutes, cool and decorate. The ears start to look like mouse ears if they're not a little smaller than the arms and legs. Roll the nose ball to make it more oval in shape and place it on the lower half of the face. These can be decorated with any icing, such as tinted royal icing made from meringue powder, to add eyes, nose, and a bow tie to each. Easter bunnies may be made using light corn syrup, not molasses. Substitute white sugar for the brown sugar. Omit spices and add a bit of almond extract if desired. Make them the same way, but make two long ears on the top and two cheek-balls instead of the nose-ball. Decorate with pastel icings.

Grandma's Best Ginger Snaps

Serves 48

Ingredients:

1	cup	packed brown sugar
¾	cup	shortening
¼	cup	molasses
1		egg
2¼	cups	all-purpose flour*
2	teaspoons	baking soda
1	teaspoon	ground cinnamon
1	teaspoon	ground ginger
½	teaspoon	ground cloves
¼	teaspoon	salt
		granulated sugar

Directions:
Mix brown sugar, shortening, molasses, and egg. Stir in flour, baking soda, cinnamon, ginger, cloves, and salt. Cover and refrigerate for at least 1 hour. Heat oven to 375F. Grease cookie sheet lightly. Shape dough by rounded teaspoonfuls into balls. Dip tops into granulated sugar. Place balls, sugared side up, about 3 inches apart on cookie sheet. Bake 10 to 12 minutes, or just until set. Place on window ledge to cool.
*If using self-rising flour, decrease baking soda to 1 teaspoon and omit salt. You can use either light or dark molasses in this recipe.

Mom's Ginger Snaps Deluxe

Serves 36

Ingredients:

¾	cup	shortening
1	cup	brown sugar
¼	cup	molasses
¼	cup	water
2	teaspoons	baking soda
1	teaspoon	cinnamon
1	teaspoon	ginger
½	teaspoon	salt
2½	cups	flour

Directions:
Beat shortening for 30 seconds. Add sugar and beat until light and fluffy. Add molasses and water. Mix well. Add the baking soda, cinnamon, ginger, and salt. Mix. Finally, fold in flour. Mix well. Form into 1 inch balls.

Place on a greased cookie sheet 2 inches apart. Flatten slightly and bake at 375F for 8 to 10 minutes. Place on window ledge to cool.

Grandma's Oatmeal Cookies

Serves about 24

Ingredients:

1½	cups	brown sugar
½	cup	lard
2	cups	rolled oats
2	cups	flour
1½	cups	seedless, chopped, raisins
5	tablespoons	sour milk
2		eggs
1	teaspoon	baking soda dissolved in 3 teaspoons hot water
1	teaspoon	nutmeg

Directions:
Combine ingredients. Drop by spoonfuls onto cookie sheet. Bake at 375F until knife can be inserted and removed without wet dough visible.

Easy Peanut Butter Cookies

Serves 24 to 48

Ingredients:

1¼	cups	flour
¾	teaspoon	baking soda
¼	teaspoon	salt
½	cup	margarine (1 stick)
½	cup	peanut butter
½	cup	sugar
½	cup	packed brown sugar
1		egg
½	teaspoon	vanilla

Directions:
Stir together flour, baking soda, and salt. In a mixer bowl beat butter for 30 seconds. Add peanut butter and sugar. Beat until fluffy. Add egg and vanilla and beat well. Add dry ingredients to beaten mixture and beat until well combined. Shape dough into 1 inch balls and roll in granulated sugar, if desired. Place 2 inches apart on an ungreased cookie sheet. Crisscross with the tines of a fork dipped in water. Bake at 375F for 9-10 minutes. Cool about 1 minute before removing to a wire rack. For an alternative, do not crisscross with a fork. Simply cook as directed. Upon removing cookies from the oven, place a chocolate candy kiss in the center of each cookie, unwrapped of course. Press slightly and cool completely. You can also wrap cookie dough into a 1 inch ball around a candy kiss and cook as directed. This gives you a cookie with a chocolate center.

Mom's Best Raisin Cookies

Serves 24
Ingredients:

1	cup	brown sugar
1	cup	water
2	tablespoons	shortening
1	cup	raisins
½	teaspoon	salt
1	teaspoon	baking soda
1	teaspoon	cinnamon
1½	cups	flour
½	teaspoon	ginger

Directions:

In a pot, combine the sugar, water, raisins, shortening, and salt. Stir over a gentle heat until the sugar and shortening have melted. Raise heat and bring to a boil, stirring continuously. Simmer for 1 minute. Remove from heat and cool. Sift dry ingredients in a mixing bowl. Add the cooled mixture and mix well. Drop by teaspoonfuls onto a cookie sheet. Bake at 350F for 15 minutes.

Mom's Oatmeal Cookies

Serves 30
Ingredients:

¾	cup	butter flavored shortening
1¼	cups	firmly packed light brown sugar
1		egg
½	cup	milk
1½	teaspoons	vanilla
3	cups	oats (not instant oatmeal)
1	cup	all-purpose flour
½	teaspoon	baking soda

½	teaspoon	salt
¼	teaspoon	cinnamon
1	cup	raisins
1	cup	coarsely chopped walnuts

Directions:

Heat oven to 375F. Grease baking sheet with butter flavored shortening. Combine butter flavored shortening, light brown sugar, egg, milk, and vanilla in large bowl. Beat at medium speed of electric mixer until well blended. Combine oats, flour, baking soda, salt, and cinnamon. Mix into creamed mixture at low speed just until blended. Stir in raisins and nuts. Drop rounded tablespoonfuls of dough 2 inches apart onto baking sheet. Bake at 375F for 10 to 12 minutes, or until lightly browned. Cool 2 minutes on baking sheet. Remove to kitchen counter.
You may omit the raisins and nuts. Bake and cool. Microwave 1 cup fudge frosting for 20-25 seconds, or until smooth and thin. Dip top half of cookie in frosting. Lay on waxed paper until set. Another variation is to omit the raisins and nuts, and add 1 cup of baking chips to batter (see picture, below). Bake and cool. For maple-walnut cookies, omit the raisins and add 1½ teaspoons of maple flavoring to batter. Bake and cool. Frost top of cooled cookie with mixture of 1 container of vanilla layer cake frosting and 1 teaspoon maple flavoring. Garnish each with a walnut half.

Grandma's Macaroons

Serves 24

Ingredients:

2			egg whites, room temperature
½	teaspoon		vanilla (or almond) extract
	2	tablespoons	flour
	½	cup	sugar
	¼	teaspoon	salt
	2	cups	flaked coconut

Directions:

Preheat your oven to 325F. Lightly grease and flour 2 large cookie sheets. Set aside. In large mixing bowl, beat egg whites until stiff but not dry. Beat in vanilla. Mix together remaining ingredients. Fold into egg whites. Drop by rounded teaspoonfuls onto prepared cookie sheets 2 inches apart. Bake 20 to 25 minutes, or until golden brown. Cool slightly, then remove.

Mom's Raisin Oatmeal Cookies (combine the two recipes above).

Cornflake Macaroons

Serves 24

Ingredients:

2		egg whites
1	cup	sugar
½	teaspoon	vanilla
1	cup	coconut
2	cups	cornflakes
½	cup	nuts, chopped

Directions:
Beat egg whites until stiff and dry. Fold in sugar gradually. Add vanilla, coconut, cornflakes, and nuts. Drop by the teaspoonful onto a well greased cookie sheet. Bake in 325F oven until light brown.

Mom's Macaroons

Serves 6

Ingredients:

2		egg whites
¼	teaspoon	salt
¾	cup	sugar
½	teaspoon	vanilla
1	cup	cornflakes
2	cups	shredded coconut

Perfect macaroons, fresh from mom's oven.

Directions:
Preheat your oven to 300F. Beat egg whites with salt until shiny peaks form. Add sugar gradually and beat until very stiff. Add vanilla to above. Fold coconut and cornflakes into egg white mixture. Drop onto greased cookie sheet. Form into mounds. Bake 20 minutes. Remove from cookie sheet at once.

Mom's Minty Macaroons

Serves 48

Ingredients:

3		egg whites
¼	teaspoon	cream of tartar
¼	teaspoon	salt
¾	cup	sugar
¼	teaspoon	peppermint extract
2	cups	flaked coconut
1	package	(6 ounces) semisweet chocolate chips

Directions:
Heat oven to 300F. Grease cookie sheet lightly. Beat egg whites, cream of tartar, and salt in medium bowl until

foamy. Beat in sugar, 1 tablespoon at a time. Continue beating until stiff and glossy. Do not underbeat. Fold in peppermint extract, coconut, and chocolate chips. Drop mixture by the teaspoonful about 2 inches apart onto cookie sheet. Place a chocolate chip on each cookie. Bake 20 to 25 minutes, or just until edges are light brown. Cool 10 minutes. Remove from cookie sheet.

Old-Fashioned Brownies

Serves 10

Ingredients:

¼	cup	oil
1	teaspoon	vanilla
1	tablespoon	white vinegar
1	teaspoon	baking soda
1	cup	white sugar
2	tablespoons	cocoa powder
½	teaspoon	salt
1½	cups	white flour
½	cup	walnuts, chopped

Directions:

Mix together the oil, vanilla, vinegar, and cold water. Add the baking soda and mix well. Beat in the sugar, cocoa powder, and salt. Finally, fold in the flour. Mix only enough to ensure that the ingredients are well blended. Pour into baking dish. Bake for 30 minutes at 350F. When cool, cut into squares.

Mom's Special Caramel Brownies

Serves 25

Ingredients:

14	ounces	caramels
¼	cup	evaporated milk
8	ounces	German sweet chocolate
6	tablespoons	butter
4		eggs
1	cup	sugar
1	cup	flour (sifted)
1	teaspoon	baking powder
½	teaspoon	salt
2	teaspoons	vanilla
6	ounces	chocolate chips
1	cup	chopped walnuts

Directions:

Preheat your oven to 350F. Grease and flour a 9 x 13 inch baking pan. Combine caramels and evaporated milk in top of double boiler over low heat. Cover and simmer until caramels are melted, stirring occasionally. Set aside, keeping warm.
Combine German sweet chocolate and butter in 2 quart saucepan. Place over low heat, stirring occasionally, until melted. Remove from heat. Cool to room temperature. Beat eggs until foamy using electric mixer at high speed. Gradually add sugar, beating until mixture is thick and lemon colored.
Sift together flour, baking powder, and salt. Add to egg mixture, mixing well. Blend in cooled chocolate mixture and vanilla. Spread half of mixture into prepared baking pan. Bake for 6 minutes. Remove from oven and spread caramel mixture carefully over baked layer. Sprinkle with chocolate chips. Stir ½ cup of walnuts into remaining chocolate batter. Spread batter by spoonfuls over the caramel layer. Sprinkle with remaining nuts.

Bake for 20 minutes. Cool in pan on rack. Refrigerate before cutting into bars or squares. These brownies are very difficult to cut if not chilled first.

Fudge Brownies

Courtesy of The Wheat Foods Council
Serves 20

Ingredients:

1¼	cups	margarine
2	cups	sugar
2	teaspoons	vanilla
½	cups	nuts (optional)
4		eggs
1½	cups	flour
¾	cup	cocoa

Directions:

Melt butter and add cocoa. Stir in sugar. Blend in eggs, one at a time. Add vanilla. Stir in flour and nuts; mix well. Bake in greased 9 x 13 inch pan for 30 minutes at 350F. Let cool on rack for 20 to 30 minutes. Cut into 20 square pieces.

Mom's Marshmallow Bars

Serves 10 to 12

Ingredients:

2	ounces	unsweetened chocolate
½	cup	butter
1	cup	sugar
2		eggs
½	cup	flour
1	teaspoon	vanilla
1	cup	chopped pecans
16		large marshmallows

Directions:

Preheat oven to 350F. Grease an 11½ x 7 inch baking pan. Melt chocolate and butter in top of double boiler over hot water. Set aside.
Cream sugar and eggs until light and fluffy. Add flour. Beat. Add melted chocolate and butter. Beat well. Mix in vanilla and pecans.
Pour into prepared pan. Bake 18 minutes. Remove from oven and cover with marshmallows. Return to oven and bake until marshmallows are lightly browned.
Cool slightly and cut into bars.

Index